WHY I AM A PREACHER

Why I Am a Preacher

A Plain Answer to an Oft-Repeated Question

BY
ULDINE UTLEY

Introduction by
BISHOP EDWIN H. HUGHES
Methodist Episcopal Church

WIPF & STOCK · Eugene, Oregon

Wipf and Stock Publishers
199 W 8th Ave, Suite 3
Eugene, OR 97401

Why I Am a Preacher
By Utley, Uldine
ISBN 13: 978-1-4982-9439-3
Publication date 5/30/2016
Previously published by Garland Publishing, INC., 1931

TO

*MY DEAR MOTHER AND DADDY
WHOM I COUNT MY
BEST FRIENDS*

INTRODUCTION

I AM asked to write an Introduction to this volume prepared by my young friend, Uldine Utley; and I comply gladly. The peculiarities that the book naturally suggests are two:

I. Uldine Utley is a woman-preacher. I can myself recall the first woman-preacher I ever saw, —far back in the eighties of the last century. Her name was Mrs. L. O. Robinson, and she hailed from Indianapolis. She was remarkably ready in speech and persuasive in all her dealings with an audience. A preacher of her sex was in those days a genuine curiosity. People crowded the churches in which she preached that they might see and hear her; and, as her sex was an advertisement, so her sermons became an even more effective advertisement. It was impossible for the conservative to lift up abstract arguments as against the concrete certainty that this feminine herald of Christ was assuredly doing His work. Coming in doubt, they went away with the feeling that the stilling of that voice by an ecclesiastical edict would somewhat resemble a sin against the Holy Spirit.

In that distant time the matter was hotly debated! I can recall that Miriam the prophetess and Deborah the prophetess, both so-called in the Bible, were summoned for a virtual testimony. I did not then know of other examples,—Huldah and Noadiah in the Old Testament, and Anna in the New Testament; nor had I heard of that strange passage in Revelation where one of the accusations against the dreadful Jezebel was that she "called herself a prophetess"! It is rather a wonder that some conservative exegete did not use that reference! Thus, long ago, conservatism had a difficulty in dealing with these Biblical examples. The greatest of the prophets speaks of his wife as a prophetess! More than one modern prophet could go and do likewise!

But the living arguments for women-preachers seem to have won the day measurably,—if not wholly. At any rate, the matter is no longer debated with much feeling,—as to the main thing. The controversy now touches only details and deals with the ways in which a public ministry could be maintained by a mother, or with similar questions. Maude Royden preaches in conservative England, while in America the mere fact that the preacher is of the gentler sex is no longer an advertisement because of novelty. Uldine Utley belongs to an increasing group. By the time she came into the fellowship of Anna and Miriam, the people, for the most part, had joined Moses in saying—"Would God that all the Lord's people were prophets!"

II. The larger objection to Uldine Utley's preaching has been on the basis of age rather than of sex. The Scriptural examples here were not so many nor so convincing. But Naaman's little Hebrew maid did some service. General statements, like "a little child shall lead them," did not suffice; and they were prophecy rather than precedent. Moreover, this girl-preacher appeared just when our land was having a heated controversy over child-labor! We were sometimes asked whether the objection to placing adult work into young hands or upon young shoulders did not apply to evangelism? Yet I have felt that this special case bore God's credentials. Uldine Utley, as a child, remained a child. She was a good example of what St. Paul says in his great love chapter,—she thought and talked "as a child." Her parents and friends did not force maturity upon her. She did not become an old woman while still being a little girl. She was no tiny scold, nor infantile lecturer. God mercifully saved her from the excesses that would have made her abnormal.

Therefore, she was likewise saved from a disastrous reaction. Dickens tells us of a boy—named Toots, was he not?—who was stuffed with knowledge prematurely and who suffered a pitiful rebound, ceasing "to have brains" just when brains would appear to be most in order. Quite often infant prodigies do not fulfil their promise. Once I heard a preacher say that his most perilous period was when he was a "boy-preacher"; and that only the wisdom of a mature clergyman saved him from a terrific relapse into a kind of permanent infanthood! But wise hands guided Uldine Utley through this period; and she has steadily grown and gone forward! As she has advanced in years the solidity and seriousness of her work have proved as effective in drawing-power as did her youth.

In this volume she tells her story,—tells it with appealing interpolations; tells it with lovely departures into exhortation; tells it with the simplicity that belonged to her girlhood and with the understanding that belongs to her advancing womanhood. I pray God that the book may have a truly evangelistic mission, even as its young author has: and, as I introduced her through the prints to the Chicago public when she received her Preacher's License in Thoburn Church, Chicago, so do I now introduce her story to a public wider than that of Chicago,—in the hope that these printed leaves may be for the healing of the nations.

EDWIN HOLT HUGHES.

Chicago, Ill.

PUBLISHER'S FOREWORD

THE purpose of this book is not to give a detailed account of the evangelistic campaigns in which Uldine Utley has engaged, nor the results of them. Rather (as the title of the book suggests), it is intended as a sincere testimony to the saving and keeping power of Jesus Christ.

Ever since the very first services conducted by the young evangelist, people have kept asking her, "Why are you a preacher?" desiring to hear the whole story. No service was devoted to telling it, however, until October 31, 1926, when, in Madison Square Garden, New York City, following four weeks of meetings held in Calvary Baptist Church, the story was told and the question answered.

Immediately afterward, a large number of requests were received, asking if it were possible to secure in print that which had been heard from the platform of Madison Square Garden. These requests have continued to be made and it has been deemed fitting to record in this volume the service as it was conducted and the story as it was told, on that occasion. The past remaining unchanged, there is no necessity for the testimony given in the Garden to be altered for the printed pages, the compilation of which follows the stenographic notes of the recording secretary.

Some of the campaigns conducted since that time and which bring events up to the present date are summarized briefly in these pages, to which are added several Gospel messages, by special request.

To repeat: this volume is issued in deference to many persistent requests from those who either heard the story at Madison Square Garden or were told of it. It goes forth accompanied by the sincere hope that genuine and lasting spiritual benefit may accrue to many readers, by its being given to the public in its present form.

CONTENTS

PAGE

I

WHY I AM A PREACHER 13

1. THE SERVICE IN MADISON SQUARE GARDEN

The Story Begins—Then Something Happened!—A New Uldine Utley—A Different Home—Filled with the Spirit—Uplifted Hands!—The Vision of the Rose—After That—Testifying Again—A Definite Call—"Uldine Will Remain After School!"—Christmas, 1923—Campaign Results—How the Magazine Started—Invited to New York City—A Prophecy Fulfilled.

2. WHAT HAS HAPPENED SINCE

In Churches—Special Meetings.

II

GOSPEL MESSAGES 97

1. ROSE OF SHARON
2. THE RIGHT OF WAY
3. THE CHRIST OF THE MASSES
4. ADRIFT

I

WHY I AM A PREACHER

1. The Service in Madison Square Garden

STRETCHING out before me into an indefinite ocean of faces, sit fourteen thousand people. They are strangers to me, and have seemed to come from nowhere into here. Outside the rain is beating down upon this great metropolis in torrents and the streets in some places seem almost rivers. Yet here, in the new Madison Square Garden, people are singing songs of praise and the choir of hundreds of voices rises behind me like some huge mountain, it seems to me. And oh, how they do sing! The song which sounds the best to me when they sing it is the campaign chorus:

In my heart there rings a melody,
There rings a melody with heaven's harmony;
In my heart there rings a melody;
There rings a melody of love.

Certainly that melody rings in my heart today, the melody of Jesus' love. It is all so much of a miracle to me: these fourteen thousand faces, these exultant voices of praise, these "Amens" I hear. A miracle because I realize it is all the working of my Saviour whose love fills my heart with melody today. It has been no working of mine, for the

Bible says, "Not by might, nor by power, but by my Spirit, saith the Lord of hosts."

It was His Spirit that directed my footsteps to a place of revival where I was saved, His Spirit that revealed to me my call to proclaim the unsearchable riches of Christ, and His Spirit which has kept me in His work with such constancy that, during the past three years, from the Pacific Coast to the Atlantic, and now into the heart of New York, I have come with such rapidity that I have hardly realized just what the Lord did have on the other side of tomorrow.

But now I know what happens during yesterday's tomorrow, for the faces before me bring me back from my dreaming and seem to say, "We are here because we want to know what *God* has done. Tell us of Him, His power, His love." Praise His Name, that is just what I want to do! The four weeks of revival in Calvary Baptist Church are ended, this is the closing service, held here under the auspices of the Evangelistic Committee of New York City, and it had been announced that I would give them my personal testimony.

After an opening prayer by Dr. Arthur J. Brown, General Secretary of the Presbyterian Board of Foreign Missions, and a word of thanksgiving to God for His gracious revival by Dr. John Roach Straton, Mr. William G. Pigueron of the Evangelistic Committee of New York City stands to his feet and I realize that he is about to introduce me. During the joyous clapping of many hands there is one thought which enters my consciousness, and remaining there, excludes all else. It is this: "I must introduce Jesus to the unsaved among these people, by telling them what He has done for me, and by showing His willingness to do as great things for them, make Him as real to them as He is to me."

Upon rising to the higher platform at the front of the stage to face the tiny microphone and the vast throng stretching away beyond it, I forget faces, and voices and all else except this, "I am speaking for my Saviour today."

* * * *

The Story Begins

You are here today and I am here, yet the presence of One who is here means more than even your being here or my being here—this One is Jesus. It is my desire to introduce Him to you through His dealings in my life, that you who as yet do not know Him in His saving fulness may so know Him today, before you leave Madison Square Garden.

Perhaps this testimony should begin at the beginning, which was, to be exact, March 16, 1912, when I was born in Durant, Oklahoma, the first child of Mr. and Mrs. A. H. Utley. I am not concerned, nor are you, I am sure, regarding the events of the first few years, although I may say that my first memory is of the treeless plain on which we lived in the southeastern part of Colorado, and of the little dug-out (as they were called) which was our home.

I remember the big sky—it seemed so much bigger than the one we just now and then get a glimpse of in New York—and the feeling of loneliness and isolation that I had all the time we lived there, for we were eighty-five miles from even a railroad and, sometimes, Daddy was gone for two or three days at a time, bringing food from the cities for the little village-store in Utleyville.

Then came a glad day when we moved to California and lived on a raisin-ranch near Fresno. One could not help but enjoy the California sunshine and fruit—I even liked the invigorating walk to school, and the walk home along the deserted country road. Plenty of play, plenty of grapes and figs, plenty of laughter, and then the sunset, equally beautiful as the sunrise. Then lessons to be learned indoors, and bedtime. But there were plenty of thoughts and imaginations to go with the plenty of other things. When I say plenty, I do not mean money, for I should not be truthful if I pictured plenty of that. Yet, our lack of plenty of money and our possession of plenty of everyday things to enjoy did not hinder the thoughts I desired to think.

WHY I AM A PREACHER

Being in California—where Hollywood was!—helped me greatly in deciding what I intended to do as soon as ever I could. All the day I wanted to dance and play "theatre" or the like, for what was there to hinder me? 'Way back in Colorado, even before seeing the beautiful theatres of California, or hearing about movie actresses, had I not sung and danced for my own entertainment (no one else could have possibly been entertained, I am sure!)? My ambition was, of course, indefinite except in my own mind, for I could not expect much encouragement from Mother and Daddy when their daughter wanted to be a dancer on the stage or a star on the screen—it didn't matter much to the daughter which. Even Grandmother Utley had remarked—so Mother tells me now—that when I had reached the mature age of two and a half she was afraid I was going to be an actress. I've found out since, however, that even the dear old "Hard Shell" Baptists with their slogan, "What is to be will be"—my grandmother was one—are glad when that which seems inevitable is avoided!

But I didn't know it was going to be avoided. Moreover, although I had taken no dancing lessons, I managed somehow to hold the continued interest of the school children at recess-time, dancing for them under the pavilion. My people have always been fond of music. I can remember out in the Colorado plains when Daddy took his guitar or violin or banjo—most of the time it was a guitar—and played for Mother to sing, *'Neath the Shade of the Old Apple Tree,* or *When You Wore a Big, Red Rose,* or, *Kentucky Babe.* I think Mother used to sing that because Daddy was a Kentuckian! There were other times, when Daddy would sing, too—funny little "coloured songs," that always pleased Ovella and me (Ovella is my little sister, born in Colorado, July 4, 1916). What I was going to tell you was that we bought a phonograph (by instalments, of course) and had music at home most of the time. So, you see, I had fun dancing to the accompaniment of the records.

Daddy and Mother saw my increased interest in things of that sort and failed to be enthusiastic, but I don't suppose that they could think of a way to keep me from being interested, since so many friends encouraged me and said that some day I would do what I wanted to do then. Mother didn't want me to be rebellious (I know that was her reason) so she allowed me to join a school dramatic club and I knew I would have "just a lot of fun." I went, I guess, about three times, not more.

Then Something Happened!

I hadn't known, of course, that it would happen, but it did, and oh, I've been so glad ever since.

I was converted!

By that I mean I was genuinely saved, my heart cleansed from all sin by the precious blood of Jesus. Listener, do not forget that the child as well as the man needs the Saviour. When we come to the age of accountability, that of knowing right from wrong, we come also to a place of judgment and decision. We are all sons of Adam and, therefore, "death passed upon all men," and the "Adam" nature influences us in the wrong direction and we can never hope for salvation by our own works. But there is a second Adam (I Cor. 15: 45, 47). Hallelujah! Through the disobedience of one many suffered, yet through the obedience of one Man, even Christ, the second Adam, many shall be made righteous. This change that takes place in the heart and life by accepting Christ is called the new birth (read John 3: 1–7). We are born into the world sinners, we are born again (becoming members of the Church, Heb. 12: 23) when Christ becomes our Saviour by the act of our faith in His redemptive work and our acceptance of His shed blood as the only way of our deliverance from sin and its wages, death.

And I was really born again. There was no doubt in my mind at the time of my conversion nor is there today, nor will there be tomorrow, for as the Scripture says, "The Spirit itself beareth witness with our spirit, that we are the children of God" (Rom. 8: 16).

But let me tell you the details:

You will recall the Junior Dramatic Club I told you about a moment ago, which Mother let me join? Did I tell you that the director gave me the leading rôle in the play they were to introduce at the first of the season in one of the Fresno theatres? Well, he did, to my astonishment, although I had been there but three times. So you can imagine I was very excited. It was to be such a big event, and I was to do what I wanted to do so long! The story I was to play in was explained to me partially, although I was to receive my part on the next afternoon of rehearsal, which was Saturday.

The story had in it a little girl who was very poor and it was this part I had been chosen to play. She was shunned by her playmates and was very melancholy because of her poverty, when she had so many golden dreams that it seemed could never come true. Then the father of the little girl "struck oil" in Oklahoma, or some other oil-field, and she was rich. The closing scene was that of the little girl skipping down the village sidewalk, under the trees, in a new fluffy dress with just lots of frills and ribbons, while the other children looked up from their play in amazement. What had happened? "My father is rich," the little girl was to say in happy explanation.

And that was the end of the story. But the little girl called Uldine Utley did *not* take the part,

WHY I AM A PREACHER

although she found that her heavenly Father was very rich, and that these riches were hers.

You see, it was Saturday, the day I was to get my part to practise; the director had said so, adding that he was counting on me, which, of course, made me all the more anxious to do my best. Grandpa Bray (Mother's father) lived with us in Fresno (I forgot to tell you we lived in town now, but moved out to the country later). Grandpa took me to the clubrooms and turned the doorknob to go in. It would not open. He turned harder, shook it. It was closed and locked. I kicked it, "I must get in," I cried. Grandpa reasoned, "If the door is locked this is not the day to practise . . . there would be lots of children here." "Yet this *was* the day," I frowned.

"But we can't help it now," concluded Grandpa, philosophically, "and I am going to a revival meeting in the Civic Auditorium. You might as well come with me." I protested, declaring that I didn't care anything about church, anyway, and that Sunday School once a week was too often as it was, and that nine-year-old girls couldn't possibly understand a sermon, or care to, either, for that matter. But, of course, we went.

Grandpa sat on one side of the building, and I on the other, in order to get seats at all, for the place was filled. The afternoon sermon was about David and Goliath. The evangelist said that each one of us ought to have as much faith in God as the little shepherd boy had, regardless of the power of Goliath (who represented the devil's power and threatenings). Also, that if we would give our lives to Jesus to be His followers we would have worthwhile influence in the world, and no matter how little we were, or young, or unlearned, or how many obstacles were in our way, we would know victory as David knew it when he said to Goliath, "You come to me with your spear and with your shield, but I am come in the name of the Lord of hosts, the God of the armies of Israel, whom thou hast defied."

The Holy Spirit seemed to burn each word into my heart. Had I said that a nine-year-old girl could not be interested in what a preacher had to say? Then I had been wrong. I listened to every word that was spoken, feeling as I might have felt had I lived in Galilee two thousand years ago when the Peasant-Prophet, Jesus, drew little children to His side and laid His hand upon their heads and blessed them. I know that Jesus really did lay His hand upon me then. How else can I explain to you the reason that I sat there with tears in my eyes as I heard the sermon?

"There is nothing to cry about like this, and in public, too," I thought, desperately trying to wipe away the tears.

My heart was touched by the power of the Holy Spirit and I wept for the same reason that thou-

WHY I AM A PREACHER

sands before me have wept when they came face to face with such a Saviour as Jesus. I felt keenly my need of Christ. This was not of my own reasoning, naturally, for I had never thought about it before. It was the blessed Spirit of God wooing me unto the only One who could make my life what it really ought to be.

I raised my hand for prayer—not very high, I admit—and then put it right down again. But I found myself not only standing but out in the aisle facing the altar, being drawn to it as definitely as though the nail-pierced hand of Jesus were drawing me. The aisle was a very, very long one —it seemed to me, at least three blocks long! To make it harder, a woman sitting on the last seat of the row, right next to the aisle, turned to the man next to her, and nudging him with her elbow, said, "There goes a little girl. I wonder if she knows what she's doing."

I walked faster after that, and fell on my knees at the altar, weeping aloud and *really praying*. I had never prayed before. Of course I had said prayers. Mother had seen to that. Every night my little sister, Ovella Mae, and I would kneel down by the bed and say,

> *Now I lay me down to sleep,*
> *I pray the Lord my soul to keep,*
> *And if I die before I wake,*
> *I pray the Lord my soul to take.*
> *God bless dear Daddy, and dear Mother, and everybody all over the world. Amen.*

(Certainly I never knew that I would ever have such an interest as I now have in God blessing "everybody all over the world." But that is the way God works, isn't it? In mysterious ways, His wonders to perform. They *have* been mysterious ways to me but they have also resulted in wonders, praise His dear Name!).

That afternoon at the altar, I did not say any prayer that Mother had taught me. There is a difference, you know, in saying prayers and praying prayers. Some learn some lovely bit of poetry, some beautiful thought, and repeat to their God— the God of the Universe—as though He had never heard it before. Oh, listener, prayer means more than that! I found it out when I was nine years old and knelt at a wooden altar-bench and really prayed. I talked to the Lord. I told Him how sorry I was for the many things I had done wrong which seemed to be not only many but very wrong when I came to tell Jesus about them. I told Him many things, especially that I wanted all my life to be His disciple and always to please Him.

And, He really heard me when I prayed for pardon. He saved me out of all my sins—including those I would have committed in the future had He not saved me, then! He put a joy in my heart I had never known before. The joy from which service begins! I am so glad Jesus saved me that day! And, I want to tell you who are here in Madison Square Garden today, that I *knew* that Saturday afternoon five years ago that I was a Christian. I believed that Jesus was the Saviour of the world, I prayed that His precious blood might flow over my heart and take all my sins away—and I believed that He did what I asked Him to do. For, in salvation, faith comes first and then feeling. We believe, then we *know* that He saves us.

I felt so different when I stood up again by the altar. I knew that I *was* different than before. A woman stepped up to me, and bending over, looked into my face and said kindly, "Little girl, what are *you* going to do for Jesus?" I thought for a minute, and then said, "I'm only a little girl, I know, but I *am* going to be a little David and fight old Goliath." You see, I didn't know then that it would be so hard or that doing it would bring me here, into the heart of the world. But I am glad now that it *was* hard and that I am here.

A New Uldine Utley

It was a new Uldine Utley who met her Grandpa outside the Civic Auditorium and said, "I am glad you brought me here." That was the beginning of a long line of changes. My likes and dislikes were all different. Very truly is it said of those who are converted unto God, "The things we once loved we now hate, the things we once hated now we love."

Mother was at that service, too, and she went home with Grandpa and myself. It was not unusual for Mother to be at the revival meeting, or for Grandpa or Daddy either, for that matter. It seemed to me that they almost lived there during the entire campaign. And that was what I had wondered about before I had been saved myself—Mother and Daddy being so interested in church! I could not remember any previous time when they had been interested to this extent. Daddy's religion seemed to consist of raisins and irrigation ditches, Mother's of a garden and housework, coupled with trying to make two little girls better, of course.

My parents had been church members, but evidently their membership dated to a far distant past, and didn't bother them much. Nor did the Bible, which was more a part of the furniture in the house than of the atmosphere of the home. But I found out something that afternoon after my conversion. Mother told me that both she and Daddy had "been brought back to the Lord" during that meeting and that they, too, intended living a Christian life instead of merely *hearing* people talk about it. Grandpa Bray was also saved during the revival.

"I don't feel like I did before, Mother," I said, "and I'm going to learn all I can about the Bible. I'm more interested in that now than being an actress."

MR. AND MRS. AZLE H. UTLEY, PARENTS OF THE YOUNG PREACHER

All Mother replied was, that she was glad, or something of that kind; but there was not then, and never has been any holding back or pushing me forward, on the part of my parents. They have both "left me with the Lord" and I am glad for that.

A Different Home

Our home was different, too. The Bible was an open book now, no longer laid upon the table undisturbed. Daddy read out of it to us all—oh, how we enjoyed hearing Daddy read the Bible! Then we would all kneel down and pray. The four in our family—Mother, Daddy and we two children—seemed all to be happier. The Bible read aloud makes so much difference in a home.

Like old, dead leaves dropping off to make room for new green ones, my ambition for worldly fame just "dropped off." I wakened up to the fact one day when Mother and I, walking down the street, were overtaken by the Director of the Dramatic Club, who urged Mother to bring me back again.

"Uldine," Mother asked, "what do you want to do about it?"

"I'm afraid I don't want to do anything about it," I answered.

"You're not coming back?" asked the Director. "Just because you were converted at that *revival* meeting?" Then he said some harsh things about evangelists, adding an exaggerated statement about "this foolishness, taking a girl away from such big possibilities," and then left us abruptly.

But I hadn't found out why the door to the Clubroom was locked; afterward, however, I found out it was because the announcement about the change of address for the place of rehearsal had been lost in the mail and had not reached me. So the door was shut! And another door—into salvation and Christian service—was opened. I walked in through that open door and was saved. And I praise the Lord because I've been able, thus far, to stay on the inside of that door!

The school children thought I was joking when I brought my New Testament to school and preferred reading it during recess to entertaining them with my dancing. Soon they were laughing at me, having great sport by calling after me: "Preacher girl! There goes the preacher girl!" Just the same, I won my first soul for Christ on the school playground and, soon after, a Bible-study class was organized to which almost all the boys and girls of our class in the fifth grade attended.

And how I enjoyed Sunday school! It was almost unbelievable that I should have such interest in the Bible lesson or be so careful to learn the Golden Text. I was even sorry that I couldn't attend church during the week, like Mother and Daddy did. I couldn't, you see, for I was going to school every day, and when we moved out to the ranch Daddy did carpentering in town, and I

WHY I AM A PREACHER

rode in with him the seven miles very early in the morning, and waited until he was through work to come home again. So I couldn't attend church except on Sundays, but I could read my Testament which was given me at the revival meeting and sometimes on Saturdays I could attend the children's services, if I found a way to get into the city.

Filled With the Spirit

At church one Sunday night, the pastor preached on the subject of the Holy Spirit. It was a powerful, glowing message to Christian people and showed me clearly just my position as a believer. I had no doubt that I was saved, for I had experienced a "know-so" salvation. As the song says, "I was there when it happened, and I ought to know." And I *did* know. But I still longed for more—not that I do not now. I will always pity that Christian who is self-satisfied and says, "I have need of nothing." (When you go home read what Jesus says about that in Rev. 3: 14–18.)

Nevertheless, my longing for more spirituality and a closer walk with God was not as it now is. For today, although I pray for more light, I have a far more brilliant light in which to walk since the receiving of the Holy Spirit. At the time of which I tell you, I was not at all satisfied with my Christian experience. I knew I was a Christian, but I also knew I was not the kind of Christian that I really wanted to be.

"I need the Holy Spirit," I thought as the minister preached.

He quoted Jesus' words in regard to its bestowal. "He is *with* you but shall be *in* you." I immediately saw the difference. The Holy Spirit had been with me since that Saturday afternoon in January, 1921, at the Civic Auditorium but now He must come *within* me, to abide forever (John 14: 16, 17). Jesus had said, "Ye shall be baptized with the Holy Ghost not many days hence." Then, too, there was that Scripture I had read in Matthew's Gospel—the words of John the Baptist's: "There is one that cometh after me that is mightier than I. He shall baptize you with the Holy Ghost and with fire."

Then, just as Jesus had become my Saviour, so should He also become my Baptizer in the Holy Spirit. As the minister had baptized me at the baptismal font of the Christian church, so Jesus had promised to baptize His people in supernatural power and glory until they were completely submerged in the supernatural wonderment of the Holy Spirit.

I wanted this blessed baptism—wanted it as I had never wanted anything since I had first been saved. Then, too, this desire was different, somehow. It seemed to me that the success of my

WHY I AM A PREACHER

Christian life seemed to depend upon whether or not I received the Holy Spirit.

After hearing that message I made up my mind that God really wanted to give to all His people the fulness of His Spirit and power. Since I was one of His children, I was going to ask Him to give this blessed "fulness" to me, too!

In one of the last books he published before his death, Dr. R. A. Torrey said this:

"There have been four marked epochs in my Christian experience: First: when I came to know the Lord Jesus as my personal Saviour and my Lord. Second: when I discovered that the Bible was indeed the inerrant Word of God, that its statements were absolutely reliable in every respect, and that everything any man needed to know was contained in this one Book. Third: when I learned that the baptism with the Holy Spirit was for the present day and claimed it for myself. Fourth: when I came to see the truth concerning the Second Coming of Christ. The latter truth transformed my whole idea of life, it broke the power of the world and its ambition over me and filled my life with the most radiant optimism even under the most discouraging circumstances."

—(*The Return of the Lord Jesus*, pp. 20–21.)

Regarding Dr. Torrey's comment on the third epoch of his Christian experience—what he Scripturally terms the "baptism of the Holy Spirit"— I can echo a hearty "Amen" out of my own experience. But it was not only the realization that this experience was for me but the actual experiencing of it, that was an epoch in my life.

After a person has "tasted and seen that the Lord is good" (Psm. 34:8) no one can, simply by theorizing, convince him otherwise. It is so about the Holy Spirit, for only by being "filled with all the fulness of God" can one's life be brought in accord with the will of the Divine so as to know His goodness.

I will praise the Lord always for taking the promises given in the Bible about the Holy Spirit's indwelling and making them part of my experience so that I can now say: "I know this is true —I experienced it." In the words of John 3:11 —"We speak that we do know and testify that we have seen."

Uplifted Hands!

One thing I particularly noticed as a result of my wonderful baptism of the Holy Spirit was this: I became really concerned over the salvation of men and women. Of course, ever since I had been converted I had wanted other people to be, but it didn't disturb me very much if they were not. Now I felt it was *my* business as to whether they were saved or not. If they were not, and could have been through my efforts, then it was my responsibility. My desire to see others saved increased all the more when going to and from school, as I thought or prayed. I had only to close my eyes to see millions of hands stretched up to me from everywhere, it seemed—hands that were reaching for the Bread of Life. I would pray (Matt. 9: 38), "Lord, thrust Thou forth more labourers into thy harvest," yet never did I think once that I should some day be one of those labourers.

The Vision of the Rose

Another revelation from the Lord to me was when I was given a wonderful vision of the Rose.

This vision was so real to me when I beheld it that I forgot all about the old farmhouse with its rugless floors and worn stairs. We lived in the country then and after coming home from school, walking across the fields to shorten the distance, I had knelt down to pray before getting my lessons.

It was during this time of prayer, that I opened my eyes very wide only to see a mammoth rosebud before me. So clearly did I see it, and so natural did it look that I did not think it strange at all that I should see it. It was red as blood and had a perfection far removed from even the most perfect garden-rose. Somehow, it was different from other roses and I experienced the strange conviction that the Lord was near me in a fuller sense than He had ever been before, though, as yet, I only saw the rose. Presently it began to unfold, petal by petal, and every petal seemed more beautiful than the one that preceded it. So enthralled was I from the beginning that it was as though time and space did not exist. My attention was riveted upon the rose.

Now it was full-blown and I could look into the very heart of it—a flaming symbol of that wounded Heart that bled upon the Cross. I saw Jesus then, in the heart of the rose, and He was walking out of it! Coming nearer and nearer, I could almost hear His footfalls. How can I use human words to describe the Divine Christ? I can say "glory," and you will understand in some measure; or I can use the word "majesty," or "power" and so convey part of my meaning. Yet how insignificant the words seem beside the blessed Saviour Himself!

There were many things I had thought I would want to say to Jesus when I saw Him in heaven, but when He came to me in the vision awe drowned out whatever I would say. I could only weep and worship Him. I could not restrain the tears though I knew no grief, only joy. Seeing Jesus! This was more than I could ever have imagined! But why the rose? I did not know, but I was not unduly troubled for I knew the Lord Jesus had appeared to me, and He had chosen to appear from the rose and I knew that forever after roses would be the most precious to me of all flowers.

WHY I AM A PREACHER

The rose faded first and Jesus remained as He had first appeared, with outstretched hands. After a moment He, too, had gone but the vision is just as real to me, today, as it was then.

My joy was unlimited when I discovered in the Song of Solomon that He had said that He was the Rose of Sharon! He had given that Name to Himself when speaking to His Church! Then Jesus as my Saviour was also my Rose of Sharon, and every year of my Christian life should be a further unfolding of His grace and goodness and love! I began to think on these things, rejoicing in my heart constantly for what the Lord had done; and the more I have studied on the subject in the Bible, the more precious the theme has become to me. You can readily understand why the dearest of all the names of Jesus to me should be —Rose of Sharon.

The vision of the rose is still in my heart, and a wealth of gratitude besides. How I longed for more of the Lord! I had seen Him walking out of that mammoth rose, and I was determined to be faithful in service to Him, so that, some day, I might see Him in the City above. I recall a day on which the Lord spoke to me, saying— "Matthew 5:6," and I thought Mother had spoken, but she had not. I then looked up the reference, and many times since then I have pondered its meaning, "Blessed are they which do hunger and thirst after righteousness, for they shall be filled." Certainly this is true. The Lord does fill to overflowing the heart that hungers for righteousness, I'm glad I've hungered so.

Whenever the pastor gave an opportunity for Christians in the congregation who wished to give a public testimony to do so, I was always one of the first to speak. You see, the Lord seemed always to be doing something special for me, and I was always eager to tell what it was. One day, when passing on my way to school I stopped at the house of one of my school-friends so she could go along with me. Just before we started off, her mother stopped me.

"Uldine," she began, "I want to ask you something. It's about your testimony in church. It's much too lengthy. The other children, your size, do not say so much. My daughters, for instance. They say, 'I'm glad I'm a Christian,' or something as brief; but you talk as long as the grown-ups and it isn't very becoming. Don't you think so?"

I didn't say what I thought, but just nodded my head and tried to say "Yes" or "No," or whatever seemed appropriate. But my thoughts were quite different.

"I will not testify any more," I said to myself.

Queer, isn't it, that we think failing the Lord is going to make things better for ourselves?

"I will speak briefly, then," I should have said, but I did not.

The next time the pastor asked for testimonies

from the congregation I was not among those who said what the Lord had done for them.

"What's the matter, Uldine?" my little friend, Geraldine, asked me. "This is the first time in ages you haven't testified."

"Some other time I may," was my reply, "but not today," and Geraldine looked more surprised. I felt badly that I had not told what the Lord had done for me during that week, for He had really done a lot. The next Sunday my pride still had the better of me. I felt I simply couldn't stand up with that woman in the congregation and knowing what she had said to me before. So I kept my seat again, while others testified. Before three weeks had passed, I felt quite uncomfortable every time I read the Bible, and when I prayed, I felt strangely, as though there was something I should make right before I talked with the Lord.

When washing the dishes for Mother, for example, she would often find me crying and would question me if I had done or said anything I shouldn't?

"I d-o-n-'t thin-k any-th-ing's wrong!" I would sob out, in reply.

Then, coming home from school one day I threw my books on the bed and then myself, and holding my Bible, fell to praying.

"If I'm miserable, Lord, because I have not testified," I cried, "then show me that that is the trouble and I'll begin again—and more briefly."

Then I stared at the open Bible, for there I read these words: "Woe unto them that are at ease in Zion." I felt that this Scripture could mean none other than myself. I was at ease. I was not helping to win others to Jesus by giving my testimony as I had done, hitherto, and it was my own pride that was keeping me from testifying. I cried out in repentance, and promised the Lord I would do everything I could for Him from that time on, and would try and not let my pride stand in my way. I also promised Him to say less, and make what I *did* say in meeting, mean more than so many words.

The next Sunday morning's service was Communion, and when I knelt at the altar with the others to partake of the bread and wine I made a new consecration of humble service to my Master, which I am glad to say has never been broken unto this day. I have not always done as much for the Lord as I should, but at least I have tried, and am thankful for that experience. It taught me I should be humble when people say things I do not like, and while receiving correction, to be faithful in all that Jesus wants me to do.

After That

After this memorable experience I always testified, as briefly as possible, but also as faithfully, every Sunday. My reward came. An evangelistic tabernacle had been built in Fresno, and on

WHY I AM A PREACHER

Sunday afternoons the people of many denominations assembled for worship. Mother and Daddy, Ovella and I always went.

After the service, one Sunday, I saw a man and woman talking to Mother, who, I found out, afterwards, were missionaries. They had heard me tell what the Lord had done for me and they asked Daddy and Mother if I might go with them to a home at which they were going to have dinner and, afterwards, to hold a little service with the family there. They wanted me to give my testimony. After much persuasion on my part, my parents allowed me to go (my little Testament given me at the revival was now very much marked and it always went with me everywhere—to school and church alike). I was taken to this home where I found a man, his wife and eight children. Dinner was ready when we arrived, so we went immediately into the large dining room where, in the centre of the long table, a large bowl of beans had been placed with a soup-bowl and spoon at the thirteen places around the table. I was as contented as if it had been a big feast, for beans are a favourite dish of mine!

Testifying Again

In the small and rather dark parlour of the house was an old-time organ that had to be pumped energetically if played at all. We sang a hymn and prayed. I remember distinctly how the room looked with the people crowded in it, and I read from the twelfth chapter of Romans, first and second verses: "I beseech you therefore, brethren, by the mercies of God, that ye present your bodies a living sacrifice, holy, acceptable, unto God, which is your reasonable service. And be not conformed to this world; but be ye transformed by the renewing of your mind, that ye may prove what is that good, and acceptable, and perfect, will of God." If what I said could be called a sermon, then this was my first text.

The fact that, as we knelt to pray around the little old organ, the father was saved, while one little girl and two of the older boys who had never confessed Christ before did so, that day, made me think that speaking for Jesus was the greatest joy in service I could ever have.

When we returned to church that night the people with whom I had gone asked Mother's permission to let me go with them the following Friday to a little town fifteen miles away, where a religious meeting was to be held in a local church. "There you can give your testimony," they said. I had little hope, really, of Mother letting me go, for I was seldom away from home even to visit relatives or friends of the family. But I did gain permission, not only for Friday night but also for Saturday and Sunday, returning to school on Monday morning.

I was glad after school Friday that Grandpa

WHY I AM A PREACHER

Bray lived so near the school, for before I went to Sanger I simply must have Grandma sew my shoe. If you had seen my shoe with the sole almost scuffed off from it, you would have believed it needed fixing. (It is a wonder I ever had any shoes the way I ran and jumped on the school playground.) Now the shoes I'm telling you about were black, and as it happened, Grandma had only white thread to sew them with! But I didn't care; I wouldn't be noticed, I thought, just testifying, with scores of others back in the congregation. And what if I *did* have on a patched gingham dress? (It was my next-to-best dress, in any case.)

Anyway, I went. After driving fifteen miles, we came to Sanger and also to the little church. There were so many cars and wagons already drawn up that we had to park about a block away. Lots of people were outside, for the little church would not hold any more, so they couldn't get in. But the boys climbed up and sat in the windows. I wondered how *we* were going to get in! All this was very exciting to me—going away from home fifteen miles, with missionaries, and hearing a preacher I had never heard before. "Only we won't be able to get in to hear him," I thought.

But my friends seemed to know what to do. They took me straight to a door and opened it. There were eyes and eyes looking at us—at my patched dress and shoes sewn with white thread!

"And now that our little evangelist has come," the preacher was saying, "we will turn the entire service over to her." A big arm reached down and drew me to one side of the pulpit behind which I had been entirely hidden.

"This is Uldine Utley," the pastor announced—and I was standing alone!

I stood on tip-toe and reached a hymnal which lay on the big pulpit. The people must never know I didn't expect all this, and had never done it before, I reasoned desperately. I bravely lifted my voice and began.

"We will commence our service this evening by singing hymn number 157," I announced (I had no idea what song would be on page 157 but, to my pleasure, I discovered that it was one I knew and with a nod to the pianist the song service began).

After all, what did it matter that I had on a patched gingham dress and scuffed black shoes? For this one night out of all my life I was doing something for Jesus, wasn't I? Then nothing else mattered.

I don't remember the order the service followed. Certainly it must have been different from any the people had ever attended before. I do not remember the message I brought to my congregation but I *do* remember the results of it. I know I started by giving my "testimony" but I must have concluded it with words that made the

WHY I AM A PREACHER

people want to find Christ, too, for although I cannot remember one word I said, yet I remember very, very well the scene at the altar that night. It would be impossible for me to forget *that*.

A long altar stretched across the front of the church, and at it, kneeling, were scores of men and women—mostly men in overalls, farmers, some of whom had driven many miles to the service (I found out later they had announced my coming throughout the country). Whenever I think of the service, I can hear people at the altar praying. And how those big, strong men cried right out loud, and prayed God to forgive them their sins!

I had a strange feeling in seeing those people kneeling at the altar. To me, it seemed there could be no greater joy in the world winning souls for Jesus! I was sure of it when, later, those same people stood and testified of their newly found happiness, and of how Christ had come into their hearts. Their faces, too, showed that they were happy.

And I was happy! Very much so when a man in the congregation asked aloud if the little evangelist was "going to testify again." When they found I was staying until after Sunday, the garage man of the village said we could have the big garage for meetings if we wished; he could put the cars that were there elsewhere for a few days, he said.

"I'll buy a sack of sawdust," somebody declared. "So will I," cried another. "Me, too," shouted a third. "I'm off work tomorrow," a man outside yelled, "so I'll build benches." And so the offers continued.

This was after my service was all over, you know, and I had stood back to have the pastor pronounce the Benediction. But instead of pronouncing it as I expected he mentioned the offering—I had forgotten that! Anyway, after the Benediction had been duly pronounced and as the people were leaving the church, the offering was taken and to my astonishment it was for me. Thus it was that the meeting in which I expected to hear somebody preach turned out to be one in which I myself was the speaker! A speaker in a gingham dress—and ten years old, at that!

I must tell you what happened the next morning. The dear old lady at whose house the missionaries and myself were staying, insisted that I come down to the department store where she worked.

"I have something to give you," said she. Of course I was curious to know what it was, and then greatly surprised and excited, for the old lady took out a big bolt of white cotton poplin goods and held it up to me. Then she began measuring it off on the counter yardstick and talking all the while, something like this:

"I just thought, last night, thought I,"—spreading out the cloth—"the little preacher needs a pul-

WHY I AM A PREACHER 45

pit dress"—measuring off one yard—"and I'm going to make her one all in white"—measuring more. "If I know anything"—she was cutting off the material as though she did—"then you'll have use for it after you leave Sanger."

She made the dress all by hand, explaining that she had prayed for me all the time she was making it, and that there was a prayer for every stitch. It was a very religious dress, wasn't it? When she had finished it she made the nicest little speech before trying it on me:

"I have made your first pulpit dress, dearie," she said, "and you'll have many more after this one."

The old lady was a good prophet as well as a good dressmaker.

Her predictions were true, regarding the dress "helping me to testify," too, and the new white stockings and shoes helped as well. Saturday night found the big garage with sawdust on the floor and benches on the sawdust and people on the benches. There were benches before the platform, too, to serve for the altar, and there were many who kneeled at it ere the service closed, and gave their hearts to Christ.

Sunday morning, afternoon, and night, I testified, and on Monday morning I was driven into the city in time for school. But I must tell you about my first Bible; it was picked out by me during my week-end in Sanger. A group of people came to me inquiring if my little Testament was the only Bible I had? I replied that it was.

"You would like to have a whole Bible, wouldn't you?" they asked. I replied that I would. "Then bring the catalogue," ordered an old lady, "and let her pick one out."

So with a Montgomery-Ward catalogue on my lap and a circle of interested spectators around me, I read advertisement after advertisement about Bibles. In addition they brought a tape measure so that I could see how large the Bibles were, which were advertised. I picked out a great big one.

"But don't you think it's much too big for a little girl like you, Uldine?" a man asked.

"No, sir," I replied. "I don't because I'm getting one big enough to last me all my life and never wear out."

Mother was amazed when I told her the things that had happened to me and especially about the Bible. I displayed my new pulpit dress, my shoes and stockings. I had a new pair of school-shoes, too, so it didn't matter if the white thread *did* show on the others.

"And I have twenty-five dollars left over!" I told Mother. "That's to buy a suitcase so I can go back again."

And it turned out that my Uncle Frank *did* buy a suitcase with some of the money and I *did* go

WHY I AM A PREACHER

back again. That little suitcase started my living in suitcases, it seems to me.

Mother said she couldn't bear the thought of my going away again because—mothers *will* say nice things like this—"it seemed a great deal longer than four days while you were away."

So I set to work to plead all week that I might go, and the friends at Sanger pled, too; thus, when Friday night came, I found myself in Sanger in the town garage!

The third week-end after that I was not reading out of a very much-marked Testament, but out of a brand-new Bible so large and heavy that I had to hold both hands under it in order to hold it comfortably at all.

I think it was about this time that Daddy found out what was really going on. The man who owned a ranch near his was talking to him.

"Say, Utley," he said, "have you heard about the revival that's going on at Sanger?"

"No," answered Daddy, and after a polite pause continued: "Now about the raisins; have you had any trouble that way with yours lately?"

"No—not so much," replied the man. Then returning to former subject he went on, "They say the preacher is just a girl, ten years old! Queer thing, too, they say her last name's Utley."

At last it dawned on Daddy that the man was talking about *his* little girl—at least, he didn't know of there being any other Utleys in that part of the country.

"What place did you say?" he asked.

"Sanger," was the reply.

Sanger—Sanger. That sounded like the place Hattie said Uldine had gone last week—and this week, too.

"You better look into the matter, Utley," grinned the man good-naturedly, "you might get interested."

And Daddy did, so much so that that very night he and Mother drove their forty-dollar Ford to the revival meeting in Sanger! And not only did *they* come but also another carload—Aunt Sudie and Uncle Frank, my two cousins, Shelly and Mary Lou, also Grandpa and Grandma Bray. Besides, there was my Great-grandma (who, by the way, is just celebrating her eighty-ninth birthday).

When they all got to Sanger they found the daughter of the Utleys and a very conspicuous Bible taking full charge of a service in the garage, which was filled with people who couldn't have been any more curious than they themselves were. After the service they took me home. I have no remaining impression of their attitude at all; evidently they didn't say anything very much against it or I would have remembered. As for encouragement, naturally I would not have expected that, because I never thought but that that would be my last opportunity to do anything as important as that for the Lord, and I was intent on doing my best while I could. There my reasoning ended; I never thought past that point.

Examinations were coming on at school and I was not able to go to Sanger again, but I prayed as earnestly for the people of Sanger as I would have, had I been there; and I appreciated their invitation to come back whenever I could.

When school was out I went to visit my Aunt Mamie, whom I loved dearly, and we had a little vacation together at a camp in the mountains. Yet, I took time daily to read and re-read the Scriptures and I spent much time in prayer. The Lord had, in a miraculous fashion, permitted me to testify for Him in Sanger, but now my task was finished and the only thing remaining for me to do was to pray for the others who could do bigger things for the Lord than I. Understand, I never thought of preaching; such a thought had not once entered my mind. Who ever heard of a girl preaching? I had not, that was certain, and I'm sure it would have seemed even foolish, to me, to think of a little girl doing it. Why, only great, big men, who knew lots and lots of things and had studied years and years to learn them, could ever be able to please the Lord by their preaching. But wasn't it wonderful that the Lord had given me that little time at Sanger in which to testify for Him? Anybody could testify for the Lord, even if only great big men could preach!

I prayed earnestly every day for those who were working for the Saviour. Yet it seemed as though I ought to be doing something for Him myself, but I didn't see how I could. What was I to do? I could only pray, so I did that faithfully. Certainly the Lord must have looked upon me kindly in the hour when I tarried in prayer; for, one day, amidst my tears of supplication Jesus Himself met me. It was on that day He bade me go and proclaim His message, and oh, I shall never cease to thank Him that He did!

A Definite Call

One afternoon I was praying as usual, and also, as usual, praying longer than I at first intended. With me, praying had grown to be not a religious form to carry out, or a duty to be remembered daily, but fellowship with my Great Teacher, in Whose presence I had rather be than in the presence of presidents or kings. Yet, strange to say, as I prayed I forgot the things I particularly wanted to ask the Lord for, for myself, and offered my petition for others. The day of which I want now to speak was like others before it. I was pleading with tears that men and women might be saved; those multitudes whose up-reaching hands I had constantly seen. At last I ventured to ask despondently, "I don't suppose I can, but do you think I could help win them,

WHY I AM A PREACHER

Lord?" I was half afraid, yet half-impatient for His reply.

But when it came, it was so far removed from what I expected it to be, that I was dumbfounded! Can you imagine what it was? It was nothing less than the commission Jesus gave to His disciples of old: yet I heard His voice differently than did the disciples, for these words came to me from the Bible: "As ye go, preach, saying, The kingdom of heaven is at hand. Heal the sick, cleanse the lepers, raise the dead, cast out devils; freely ye have received, freely give." Through almost blinding tears I could read the words plainly and the more I looked the more stupendous they appeared to become, until they seemed to be imprinted upon my heart there to abide forever.

I dried my tears, and stood up trembling.

"I must not tell anyone," I said to myself. "None would believe me . . . and I mustn't believe it either."

But I did—almost. Do you understand me at all? *I was afraid to believe the Lord had called me to preach.* A call to preach the Gospel? Surely there was a mistake somewhere! It was too good to be true, and certainly too great to be true. How could I ever be meant to do anything so important in the world as to "carry the good tidings of great joy" unto all the people?

"I *would* if I *could*, certainly," I reasoned. "Jesus knows I would do anything that was possible for me to do. That's what I asked Him to give me, a work I could do, and I can't do this. Not in a million years!"

Mother was the only one who heard about how the call to service had come to me; I would not tell anyone else, for it was all so strange and wonderful, and so hard to understand. Yet I was forced to believe that the Lord really had called me out into active service. What I could not believe was that I was able to answer the call. That is what I meant when I told you I was *afraid to believe*. I had not yet experienced the truth of the Scripture, "He which hath begun a good work in you will perform it until the day of Jesus Christ" (Phil. 1:60). Nor did I then realize that what the Lord asks you to do for Him, He will enable you to do.

Day after day I increased in certainty, while praying; that is to say, that while upon my knees I *knew* the Lord had meant that I should receive that Scripture just as I had read it—that it *did* mean for me to preach the Gospel. But when I arose from my knees and began to reason it out in my own mind—how often we make that mistake after praying—I would increase in fear. All that I would like to do for the Lord was impossible. I simply couldn't do as He has asked me to. In the first place, I was only in the sixth school-grade. A lot I knew to tell people—I in the sixth grade! Yet the Scripture would come back to me and every day the Lord was teaching me wonderful things out of His Word. I could have said as truthfully as ever the Psalmist did: "I behold wondrous things out of thy law" (Psalm 119:18).

I felt the first part of the Scripture was correct, I had received *freely*—but here was the problem, to be able to "freely give"—to show others what the Lord had shown me (perhaps they would not think the Lord *had* shown me, I thought); to tell all the people what I had found to be precious truth in the Bible—ah! that was a very different and a very difficult thing. Only in the sixth school-grade—how could I preach? And where could I go to preach? Who would listen to me after I got there? If they would listen, what would I say? Would I not be too afraid to speak? If I should face a great audience wouldn't I be too awed to speak? When if I were really to "GO" as that Scripture had said—travel from place to place—how could I? Mother and Daddy wouldn't go with me, of that I was sure; they were too interested in their home, and Daddy would never think of quitting his work, and I couldn't go all by myself. So what was I to do?

I thought out these things in my mind, over and over again. Thoughts like these are very disturbing, you know, and to say I was miserable would not exaggerate my state of mind in the least. I walked in a sort of daze. The Lord had called me to carry His message to the people and I couldn't do it. Yet, finally it took just about five minutes to settle it . . . and, as you may imagine —it was the Lord who settled it after all.

It happened on a Wednesday night. A woman was taking me to the church prayer-meeting and as it turned out we were the only passengers on the street-car. I was weary with my reasoning; then, suddenly, I thought that the Lord did not intend me to be struggling with this problem. How utterly foolish I had been to raise any objection! Did not the Lord know what He was doing, if He called a child to preach His Gospel? And if He created this great world, He ought to be able to enable a little girl to deliver His message if she were willing to do it. The whole question seemed suddenly simplified—every wrinkle ironed out, every problem solved.

I bowed my head in the street-car, and with my Bible in hand, prayed: "I accept Thy commission, Lord," I said, "Lord, I believe. But I do ask Thee to give me a confirmation of that commission Thou didst give me before, so that when I tell people of it they may never say, 'It was by chance.' Lord Jesus, give me a Scripture that is definitely for me—that no one may doubt and that I may be strengthened when I am tried."

That is exactly the way I prayed. I had read Matt. 18:16. The Lord had given me one Scripture. Now, as a confirmation, I asked for a second. I asked the Lord to do it and believed He would. And, praise His Name, He *did!*

Today, it seems to me the same as it did then—that the very hand of God must have opened my Bible to the page and the chapter that I saw when finishing my prayer. I looked down upon my Bible which I had, as a matter of habit, brought with me. These were the words I saw, and upon hearing them you will readily see why all my fears were swept away in a moment, and why, from that time to this, I have never doubted that God enables you to do what He asks you to—providing you are willing to do it. Here are the words: "Then said I, Ah, Lord God! behold I cannot speak: for I am a child; for thou shalt go to all that I shall send thee, and whatsoever I command thee thou shalt speak. Be not afraid of their faces: for I am with thee to deliver thee, saith the Lord. Then the Lord put forth his hand, and touched my mouth. And the Lord said unto me, Behold, I have put my words in thy mouth."

These words thrill me still, even as they did when I first saw them! I never knew before that the Bible could be so *personal,* so *individual.* That which had been spoken to an Old Testament prophet hundreds of years before my time so fitted my case, that, for a moment, it seemed hard for me to believe I was reading them out of so ancient and world-wide a book as the Bible.

That night I told the people at church about the

Scripture. They looked at one another, and then at me in only half-concealed amazement, and some of them opened their Bibles. It seems strange to tell it, now, but when it was all happening it seemed a very natural thing: invitations began coming in from other churches asking me to speak for them. Realizing that I was going to school through the week, pastors and church-boards would inquire if I could not speak for them on Sundays and it was not long before I was going through the entire valley speaking Friday night, Saturday morning, afternoon and night, and Sunday morning, afternoon and night. This meant, sometimes, seven services each week-end, or at least, four or five.

Sometimes I would get to the place appointed just in time to walk on to the platform and speak. But that made no difference, for had not the Lord said: "Thou shalt go to all that I shall send thee?" And I was willing to go, neither was I ever afraid, for He had promised, "I will be with thee" and I knew He was.

Because Mother and Daddy were unable to take me themselves, they permitted me to go with some of the church people. Sixty or seventy miles after school Friday, we sometimes went; sixty or seventy miles after Sunday night service to reach home; yet my lack of a warm coat never gave me a cold. Moreover: my grades in school were better made than ever, despite the fact that I was spending all available time with my Bible, because of the week-end meetings.

"Uldine Will Remain After School!"

I remember well the time I had to stay after school; but it was over such a great, big, long old poem, anyway, and it seemed to take me such a long time to learn anything, especially poems. And I hadn't learned it. I realized that when, after stumbling through some three or four long verses I was requested to take my seat (which was so much worse, you know, than if I had taken it myself!).

It turned out as I expected. "The following will kindly remain after school, until they have both learned and recited their poems correctly," the teacher said. It was a long list of names and the very last one was "Uldine"!

Now I should not have been worried had it been any other day but Friday. But Friday it was, and that night I was to speak some fifty-seven miles distant! Even then, Mr. and Mrs. Somebody-at-the-Church would be waiting for me. About half the class was staying in. "That proves," I said to myself, "that it was a hard old poem." And I *had* studied it. Then I prayed what some people might have thought a rather funny prayer, but evidently the Lord took it seriously. I asked Him either to let me get out of having to remain after school, or help me to learn the poem in at least five minutes. Now both seemed equally impossible, so it didn't make any difference to me which happened.

"Uldine," said the teacher, "come here." From what she said, one would have thought I had prayed out loud and that she had heard me pray.

"Did you try to learn this poem?" she asked.

"I really did," I answered, and thought to myself, "Now is she going to keep me in longer for something else?"

"Would you try to have it learned for me by Monday, if I let you go today?" the teacher continued.

"Indeed, I would try," I replied.

"Then you may go," she concluded.

I could hardly believe my own ears until I walked out of the room and saw all the envious glances wasted upon me by those yet remaining. What makes the matter still more strange to me is, that, to my knowledge, my teacher never knew that I was speaking in public at all. It might interest you to know, however, that I learned my poem sometime between the five services that were conducted during that week-end.

I was joyous in service. To see men and women come forward to the Mercy Seat, in confession of Christ, has never become an ordinary occurrence with me, and I don't believe it ever will. The same happiness I had experienced at Sanger repeated itself again and again, each week-end, until my

WHY I AM A PREACHER

whole interest seemed wrapped around the one thought, "How many have accepted Christ?" It was always that way.

For one thing I am particularly thankful. Mother and Daddy did not oppose me doing what I did, and remember, I was just eleven, then. Naturally, I had never been away from home alone much before, except when visiting some relative. But because Mother and Daddy could not take me themselves, being busy and having only the forty-dollar Ford, which was, as you imagine, rather undependable, they satisfied themselves with knowing that some family, which they knew well, was taking care of me during the week-ends. I shall never cease to thank the Lord Jesus for enabling Daddy and Mother to feel the way they did about my going away those week-ends to preach, and above my love for Mother and Daddy simply because they *are* my Mother and Daddy, is my love for them because of their great understanding, and helpfulness, and encouragement, in regard to my work.

Mother and Daddy were real Christians and showed it; but, no doubt, one reason they did not worry about me unnecessarily was because they thought things would go on the way they were indefinitely; that is, we would live in our little home in the country, and I would go to school during the week and speak in churches at week-ends—and everything would be comfortable and in regular routine. But it didn't work that way, and there came a day when it was up to them to make a tremendous decision—one as big as any parents ever had to make, of that I am sure.

Christmas, 1923

It was the year 1923, and Christmas was fast approaching, and a telegram came from Oakland, California, inviting me to speak in the Civic Auditorium during my Christmas vacation. The Auditorium could be secured for five days only—December 23–27. I was out of school for five days, just these same five days, and oh, I did so want to go to Oakland! It was the first time I had five whole days at one time in which I could bring the Gospel to the people, and I longed unutterably to do it. Five whole days without school to interfere!

The invitation had come because of a very high recommendation on the part of a man in charge of the San Joaquin Valley Evangelistic Association for whom I had spoken in many cities. He had conversed (this I found out later) with this pastor in Oakland regarding an invitation for me to come. Daddy and Mother knew, of course, I wanted to go but there were certain things to consider, things I, of course, would never think of. If I had not been speaking nearly every week-end since the school-term had started, it wouldn't have been so serious a consideration. Should the only

WHY I AM A PREACHER

vacation I had out of school be taken up by going a long distance, and after getting there, by speaking on every one of the five days? There was no financial guarantee except that covering the expense of renting the hall and advertising. The whole plan was a big responsibility. Should they allow me to undertake it?

But Mother and Daddy decided in the affirmative and to Oakland we went. It was a strange and very wonderful five days to me, right at Christmas time, too, one of the best times of the year. Daddy could not understand why I did not want to go with them to look at the beautiful Christmas things in the stores—why I insisted upon staying (except when I had to go out for meals) in the hotel room which my little sister, Ovella, and I shared together. But I was so intent on doing it in order that I might read my Bible and pray, that Mother and Daddy at last gave up in despair and let me alone. But they never knew what a temptation those Christmas stores were to me!

When the man would come, at night, to take us to the Auditorium, I would see all the lighted windows; when going out to eat and for my early morning walk I would see such pretty things in the stores; even from my hotel window I could see other pretty things. But I refused to go with Mother and Daddy and Ovella during the day to look at them. And there was only one reason that led to my refusal: I was determined to do my best for Jesus those five days, and I didn't want to do anything but study and pray for the night-service. Not that I dislike pretty things, or disapprove of them—quite the contrary—but putting first things first, compelled me to think of the success of those services. I prayed the Lord to give me one hundred souls every night, and, certainly, the converts of the meetings were not far from that number.

I can vividly remember walking out on that big, big stage and facing that big, big audience! Everything was frightfully big—even the people on the platform, it seemed to me, and I felt strangely too small and out of place in all that bigness. The pulpit was big, too, and had to be removed, and my Bible was very big (but of course NOT removed!).

It must have been Christmas Eve on which the people gave me the little portable typewriter. Anyway, it was a Christmas present, and a wonderful one, so wonderful, indeed, that I lost no time at all in learning how to use it (my method, of course, but it has served the purpose!) and whenever I type off an article on my portable, I remember the first Christmas in evangelistic work and the joy that little Corona brought me.

The five days were nearly ended and invitations were coming in from other places, and I couldn't help accepting one to San Francisco in place of going back to school. I did like my school very much, and enjoyed every lesson—even arithmetic, occasionally! Yet, when I thought of how much more I could do for Jesus by speaking for Him *every night* instead of just at week-ends, I could not help but ask Him about it. Someone asked me one day if I had a private tutor? This was a great surprise to me, for, as I said, "I didn't know there were such things." That's what caused me to ask the Lord about sending me one, and when a college-graduate, who had taught school for a number of years, came to Mother and Daddy and offered her services, I was certain the Lord had answered my prayer.

Thus it was that we went to San Francisco from Oakland, and I resumed my lessons, taking up my high seventh-grade work, just as I would have done were I in school. That's what has seemed so wonderful about Mother and Daddy to me: They made a very splendid and unselfish decision when they permitted me to go on in my work, at the cost of their own interests. It seems strange to me, even now, looking back on it, that they seemed so happy in making their decision. If financial reward had been a consideration, their decision would have been differently arrived at. As it was, enough was provided through the meetings to take care of our necessities, and that was all. Living in hotels and eating in restaurants didn't appeal to us at all, after Mother's good cooking and the joy and privacy of our own home. I could see that Daddy would have felt more at home as a jeweler, optician, photographer or fruit-grower, or following any other line of work in which he had engaged during his lifetime. But this was new and strange. Accepting invitations for revival campaigns; discussing with laymen and clergymen the essential preparations of a meeting; getting out advertising; overseeing the details connected with evangelistic work. Indeed, it must have been a tremendous responsibility. But he was cheerful about it all, and Mother was just as cheerful in her work. My pulpit uniforms were always spotless, and whether I wanted to study or pray there was always Mother's insistent voice when mealtime came: "Uldine, you must have hot food—and get out in the air, too, for some exercise." Oh, undoubtedly, they're the best Mother and Daddy I ever had!

Accepting an invitation to the First Methodist Church in Santa Cruz at the end of the first week, we were obliged to remain the second because of the increasing revival fervour. From there we went to the First Baptist Church of San Jose, later, to points in the northern part of the state and, finally, into Oregon and Washington.

I remember particularly the closing night of the Chico campaign, in the old Rotunda. Previously, it had been used chiefly for prize fights; but, at the end of the two-weeks' revival, the people had

WHY I AM A PREACHER 65

grown accustomed to hearing Gospel songs sung there and prayers offered. There were many souls saved. It was after the last meeting was over and the final bills had been paid out of the last offering, that Daddy discovered, to his embarrassment, that we did not have enough money to get out of town! I say embarrassment, because Daddy always felt the responsibility of the financial side of the matter. It was only after constant pleading that he consented to giving all his time to revival work; but, of course, if Daddy had not consented to take charge of the business and campaign arrangements of the services, someone else would have had to have been secured.

But, as I started to say, we couldn't get out of town. Now this, as you may imagine, was quite serious.

"Now I *know* I'm going to get a job and nothing can stop me," said Daddy.

"But," I pleaded, "let's pray first."

I shall never forget that prayer. Daddy often prayed for the meeting, for the salvation of souls, and for the Lord's blessing upon the message I was to deliver—but Daddy praying for money! It was very strange.

Slowly he began: "Lord—we hesitate to ask this of you, but it is necessary. We must have money. If it is your will, Lord, send some in. But I'm going out to look for a job. Lord, lead me."

That was at night. In the morning, a Western Union messenger came with two hundred and fifty dollars from an elderly, retired railroad engineer who had been converted in the Santa Cruz campaign! He was then visiting in Cheyenne, Wyoming, and explained to us afterward that in the night he was awakened by the persistent thought, "The Utleys need money." That's why, on the following morning, we were able to leave Chico for Oregon!

The Oregon campaigns, despite their real success, only increased our desire to go farther East. During the first revival in Oakland, an invitation had been extended to us from the Grand Avenue Temple, a Methodist Church in Kansas City, and it seemed probable that a meeting there would be forthcoming. It was almost like following the eastern star—so definite did our leading seem.

The three services held in Grand Avenue Temple proved to us, by the response of the people in their large attendance and interest, that we were in the Lord's will. Then there came the invitation from a Presbyterian pastor in Tulsa, Oklahoma, in whose church I spoke and who made possible a very splendid campaign in a great wooden tabernacle.

Campaign Results

Then came the St. Louis campaign, and, after that, the Georgia and Carolina revivals. The mere mention of these revivals bring to my mind countless instances of conversions, and reconsecrations. The conversion of a male nurse in St. Louis was an outstanding instance during that campaign. It was a remarkable deliverance from drug addiction although the man's constant and abundant use of it had made any sort of cure an impossibility, so far as medical aid was concerned. Those who were workers in the revival remember distinctly the stately and imposing figure the man made, as he went up to the altar for prayer.

An assistant to one of the outstanding surgeons in the country, there was nothing to distress him regarding his work, except that, because of its strenuousness, he had allowed himself to rely upon dope in order to carry it on. First the man bought one book of sermons, went home and read them through, marking and remarking them. Having gotten such a blessing from them himself— he had never been a Christian although his people were—he decided the patients in the hospital should read them too. Returning to the meetings, he bought some fifty books, giving them to those in one of the hospital wards.

By this time he was so desirous of being saved that he could neither eat nor sleep, and was greatly condemned by his conscience for the use of drugs. He hired someone else to take his place, paying eighteen dollars for two hours in order to leave his work and attend an afternoon service at the revival meeting, in which he had made up his mind he would go to the altar for prayer and ask the Lord to save him.

I remember very well how Daddy and one of the workers knelt down with him to pray. But the man could hardly grasp the fact that the Lord wanted to save him.

"I am such a sinner," he kept on saying over and over, as if to himself. It was at a second service that he was able to reach through all doubts, and actually believe that the Lord wanted to save him, the same as others. His remarkable deliverance was an amazing testimony in the hospital; the doctors, with whom he had worked for so long, had to acknowledge that his salvation was a miracle.

The Georgia and Carolina revivals bring to mind the many railroad shop-meetings, under the auspices of the Young Men's Christian Association. These noonday meetings were so outstanding and created such a demand, that it was necessary, at times, to have meetings at several shops the same lunch hour, allowing us only a few minutes to get from one shop to another. The officials seemed as interested as the other men who listened. There was much talk about one shop-meeting, where the man charged with the duty of blowing the whistle, forgot to do so! There were to be two whistles—by the first I was to know I had two minutes before I need dismiss and allowing three minutes before the blowing of the second whistle. I hadn't heard the first whistle so I continued to speak. Afterwards, I discovered that the "whistleman" had become so interested in listening, he had let the time to blow the second one, go by!

The number of conversions resulting from shop-meetings are really surprising, and, until today, I conduct very few revivals without some railroad man attending the services, who was genuinely converted during those meetings in Georgia and South Carolina. Each revival campaign seems to bring some new instances to mind: the three or four young people, for instance, converted during the Savannah, Georgia, revival, have gone through Bible Training Institute, and I have had the privilege of helping in their work and on the Foreign Mission fields; the homes of those in the Roanoke and Richmond revival who had never known prayer and Bible study, where now there is a spirit of real devotion to Christ and His service—and many another. Yes, I would like to tell you about one campaign after another—one conversion after another. But most of you people have read the story of these instances in our little magazine, about which I had almost forgotten to tell you.

How the Magazine Started

The converts of every meeting we held were so anxious to "keep up" with us, as they expressed it, that they were always asking for sermons and reports of meetings, and for our future address by letter. Of course, this was impossible unless the same letter was sent to them all. And even this could not be done, unless each could share in the cost of such a procedure. Then, there were the stenographically reported messages, too; the people of cities already visited were wanting the messages delivered in future campaigns.

During the Eugene revival, one of the converts, a man of about fifty, solemnly informed me, as he straightened out a one dollar bill from the others, that he wanted to be the first name on the subscription-list, if I ever decided to publish a magazine.

"But you'd better keep it, sir," I said. "I have never thought of a magazine."

Yet from that time on the thought persisted and although it seemed a great responsibility to assume, I grew very anxious to do it. But Daddy didn't see how, at the age of twelve, I could be expected to see to the publishing of a fourteen-page magazine every month. But I knew he felt the same way about my preaching at the age of eleven. So I kept on gathering material, and knew that Daddy would look after the business side of the matter if I could only keep up the editorial side.

"Well, Uldine," Daddy said, unexpectedly, one morning, "if you still want to try out editing a magazine, I guess we have enough money to print the first number."

Oh, I was so excited! That very morning I had gotten up early and had been hard at work editing the material I already had on hand and completing several new articles. By that time my wrist was really quite "achy," and at that very moment, on my bedroom desk, was material for the first number, all completed!

So, when we got to Savannah, Georgia, Daddy took the typewritten pages to a firm of printers. The secretary, of course, had typed what I had written, and the first issue of *Petals from the Rose of Sharon* came off the press. The title of the magazine was suggested, of course, by my Vision of the Rose. Feeling that Jesus, the blessed Rose of Sharon, gives to us continually His words and messages for our every need, I regarded them as "Petals"—daily unfoldings of grace and power and peace and joy—hence the name adopted for our little magazine, now discontinued.

Every month, then, revival messages, stenographically reported, and articles by myself were printed and sent to first hundreds and then thousands of friends all over the United States and foreign countries, with a prayer that they might prove to be real "petals from the Rose of Sharon," a breath of fragrance and beauty for every soul that needed the Lord.

Thus it was, that the dollar-bill which Mr. Goodenough gave me back in Oregon, engendered the thought of a magazine that finally became a reality. It has increased from fourteen pages to sixteen, from sixteen to eighteen, and having been translated into several foreign languages by missionaries who have used it in their work, it has become, so many have assured me, a source of blessing to the peoples of many lands.

That's why, in giving my testimony today, I want to praise the Lord for the privilege of putting His Gospel into print as well as declaring it by word of mouth. He has taught me so many things in writing for the magazine—perseverance, for instance: seeing to the little details required of an editor, and concentration, enabling one to write articles on trains and in public—writing rooms, and even in restaurants! There have been many other things for which I thank the Lord about the little magazine—the many who have been saved in reading it, for instance, and those who have been encouraged, as Christians, to live closer to the Lord. I am thankful, too, for the many ministers of different denominations who have not only subscribed for the magazine, but written us of the help it has been to them in their work for the Master and the souls of men.

But enough of that. What I really started out to tell you, before I got to talking about "Petals," was that after the meeting in Atlanta, Georgia, I was invited to be a speaker at the Bible Conference at Green Cove Springs, Florida, and that that invitation was really responsible for me being in New York City.

Invited to New York City

The conference was planned as a continuous program, from early morning until the usual evening service. It was to be inter-denominational in project, although held in a Baptist Church, whose pastor being the director of the Conference had invited me. I was to speak the following morning at ten o'clock, the conference opening the evening of February 22, 1926, with addresses by Dr. T. T. Shields, of Toronto, Canada, and Dr. John Roach Straton, of New York.

We arrived late on the opening day, and I remember very well how tired I felt from continual travelling, and how gratifying the prospect of being in one place for a few days appeared. As soon as I had unpacked I found there was still some little time before the hour set for the evening service. and as I did not have to speak myself, I could spend the time in walking. The woman who was then my companion, took me for a long walk and I began to feel happy and care-free, after the confinement of the train. I remember that when we were within a block of the Church—it being dark and not many people anywhere around—I ran ahead of my companion and up to the church and waited until she walked up.

I sat down on the steps of the church, laughing and panting for breath after my recent run, when someone, bending over, searched my face and asked, "Is this the little girl-preacher?"

"Yes," I answered, realizing that I could not be looking very much like one, having run to the church and being found sitting on the steps, laughing and out of breath!

The man seemed intent upon his mission, however, and asked us if we would be so kind as to come with him, as we were wanted in the parsonage next door. We went. The pastor's wife introduced us to D. Straton, who explained that Dr. Shields' train was going to be too late to permit of his speaking that evening. "And," added Dr. Straton, "I am very anxious to hear a little girl like you preach. Would you be willing to speak, tonight, in Dr. Shields' place?"

I said something or other—I don't remember what—to the effect that I would try. So, unexpectedly, I spoke that night, reading, first, John 1:29, which pictures Jesus as the Lamb of God. And unexpectedly, I heard Dr. Straton voice his surprise when I had finished, saying that his text was to be upon the same subject, and from the same chapter!

That night, when the service was over, Dr. Straton talked to me about his little daughter,

MEETING IN MADISON SQUARE GARDEN, CONCLUDING THE FIRST
NEW YORK CITY CAMPAIGN

Catherine, who, before her death, which had occurred just a short time before, had intended being a missionary, and how that he hoped I would keep on in my work for Christ. He said, moreover, that he hoped sometime I would come to his church in New York City and conduct a revival— and that's what has happened as you see.

After the conference was over, we went to the Baptist Tabernacle, West Palm Beach, then to Indianapolis, Indiana, and directly following that, to New York for the services here last spring in Calvary Baptist Church and, later, in the tent-meetings in Queensboro, Long Island.

A Prophecy Fulfilled

That brings the story up to the beginning of the present campaign, which was September 26, 1926, and to this final service in Madison Square Garden, on this 31st day of October. But I want to tell you of one other incident which happened way out West, a few days before I went to hold my first meeting in the Civic Auditorium, in Oakland. It didn't seem of much importance then, but somehow, today, facing so many of you New Yorkers, it seems to be of great importance.

Here is the incident: A real estate man who had given up his business in order to carry on an interdenominational and evangelistic work in Fresno, came to see us just a couple of days before we left for Oakland. I had played with his children and stayed at his house often, had also brought several messages in the large tabernacle of which he was the head. He came to see us about our going away, and I remember him putting out his big arm and drawing me over to him and saying very slowly, measuring each word, "Little Preacher, do you know what is going to happen some day?"

I shook my head, and was very curious.

"Then I'll tell you," he went on, speaking more quickly now and smilingly. "The Lord has called you to take His message to the people, and, someday, He is going to take you clear into New York City, the heart of the world, and, right there, you are going to preach His Gospel."

I didn't think very much about what was said—at the time. New York City was just a big place to me about which I had studied in school. But what Mr. Frisbee said that day appears to have made of him a prophet, and I only wish he were alive that I might tell him that what he predicted has come to pass. It's really *more* than true, because I feel I'm not only witnessing for Jesus here in the heart of New York, but that, somehow, I don't know what it means regarding my future work here—but, somehow, New York has crowded itself into my heart and I think of all you thousands of people here today as being my

WHY I AM A PREACHER 77

friends. Humbly, I thank the Lord Jesus for all the things He has done for me. I do not understand them. I never shall. But I thank Him anyway, and I want to show my appreciation to Him through faithful service for all He has done for me.

Do you think I have told you why I am a preacher? I hope so, for I want you to understand why. Not because Daddy and Mother had such an ambition for me; not because there were "preachers in the family"; not because I was compelled to be a preacher for any reason but one— the love of Christ and by my love for His will and pleasure. That's why I am a preacher. That's also why I was preaching at the age of eleven instead of beginning ten years later. That, also, is why I am a preacher although I'm a girl, and some people think I'm not supposed to be preaching. That's why I was a preacher who hadn't even finished grammar school, and why I am having to keep right on studying my school-lessons, and preaching at the same time.

I am compelled to preach because of the love of Christ. He called me to preach, and I cannot fail to do what He asks. I delight too much in His will; I want His favor in my life, too much. I put up no big profession; I agree with anybody who says it is foolish for a girl to preach. I honestly believe that, and I also believe what Paul says, "It pleased God by the foolishness of preaching to save them that believe." Listen, a moment. This Scripture says God saves men by the "foolishness of preaching." Then preaching is foolish, and if a girl preaching the Gospel is more foolish than a man preaching it, why should any objection be made, if souls can be saved through the method of peaching, which is more foolish?

You smile over that thought and I smile over it too, but one thing I do not smile over and that is this: God says, He will take a worm to thresh a mountain and things that are not to confound the things that are (Isa. 41:15). He says, in Isaiah 29:14, that "The wisdom of their wise men shall perish."

I make no boast—there is nothing of which I *can* boast—"I glory not, save in the cross of Christ." I fully realize that, naturally, I do not belong on this platform, today, or before you thousands of people, as a preacher. I am not worthy of so high an honor, but although I cannot understand it He not only called me here but in the language of the Scripture, "Hither hath the Lord brought me." Praise be to His Name!

He has done so much for me. I have not told you half. Nor could I. Do you remember the assuring words of the old song?

*"What He has done for others,
He will do for you."*

WHY I AM A PREACHER

Yes, He will. Not that you should want identical experience with someone else, or ask the Lord to do exactly for you what He has done for another; but He will deal as definitely and supernaturally with your life as with anyone's else. He will make Himself real and precious to you. Soon daily communion with Him will be a necessity in your life, as indeed it should be.

Draw closer to Him today, by laying aside your doubts and fears and perplexities. Simply ask Him to help you. He will. He helped me, and He'll help you. Put away from you, today, everything that displeases Him in your life. You know quite well what it is, or, perhaps, who it is. Turn from anything that the Lord cannot smile upon and turn to Jesus, today.

> *"Ask the Saviour to help you,*
> *Comfort, strengthen and keep you,*
> *He is willing to aid you,*
> *He will carry you through."*

Will you, right now, ask Him? Let us bow our heads in individual prayer. Beginning with these sections of the main floor: let me see the hands uplifted of every man and woman who would say, "Pray for me. I want to really know Jesus as my personal Saviour." Let me see. How many? That's right—God bless you! And you, too, brother. Yes, sister, and you. And you. And this young couple, yes. That's right, brother. Others? Yes, I see four and still others.

Now in the centre sections—clear to the back of the Garden. How many will, by the uplifted hand, say, "Neither am I a Christian, but I would like to be. Pray for me." How many? That's right. Yes; many, many hands! Praise the Lord for them all! And there are still others. Yes, I can see you way back there, too. God bless you, everyone!

In the right sections now, how many want to be remembered in prayer to the end that you may be saved? Yes, brother, indeed we will pray for you; and you, too, sister. God bless you, brother, and you, and you, and you! There are too many hands to count, now; but the Lord sees them. He knows and He will hear us as we pray.

Now the first gallery, on my left, clear to the back—in every section, how many will say, "Pray for me"? That's right. Oh, so many hands! Certainly these are signals stretched out towards heaven for real help from the Lord. I do not know you people, but Jesus does, and He *is* willing to save you, make you His very own disciples this day. Praise His Name!

Now let me see the hands of all those in the right gallery, who desire our prayers. God bless you! Father, mother, son, daughter, brother, sister, husband, wife—everyone!

Behind me, now, in both galleries, who'll say, "Pray for me? I'm not saved but I want to be."

WHY I AM A PREACHER

That's right! I'm glad you want to be saved. You may be, too, this very day if you are really lifting your hand for prayer sincerely and mean business with God because you desire to be saved more earnestly than you desire anything else in the world.

Now to my left, in the top gallery—every section: How many up there will say, "I, too, want prayer that I may get right with God." Hallelujah! Many, many hands! This is a great victory for the Lord! All those hands lifted for prayer, two-four-six-eight-ten-fifteen eighteen-twenty-twenty-three-twenty-six-twenty-eight-oh, there are too many to count! But I'm glad there are not too many to be prayed for!

We're going to prayer right now, but first I mustn't forget all those sections 'way up there in the right of the top gallery. How many of you would say, "While you are praying for others, will you pray for me, too." Yes, that's right! God bless you, and you, and you, sister, too. Yes! God bless you too. God bless all of you.

Will you who raised your hands for prayer stand to your feet with me that we may pray together? Please! Thank you. Yes, way up to the top row of the gallery. Everyone. That's right. Let this be a prayer in which you all join—not one to which you merely listen. I'm going to pray for you, as I promised, but you too must pray. I can ask the Lord to help you to take your stand for Him, but it is up to you to tell Him yourself that you are willing to be a Christian.

Let us pray. Everyone in Madison Square Garden, if you've never prayed before, pray now:

Blessed Lord Jesus, we come into Thy presence at this moment. To whom else *can* we go? Thou alone hast the words of eternal life. We come, —thousands of us who have assembled to hear the words of eternal life—hundreds of us who are standing now in Thy presence—we come to Thee. Regard, we pray Thee, those who raised their hands for prayer, and who are now actually taking their stand for Thee. Wilt Thou bless them, Lord? Wilt Thou take away their sins, blotting them out as though they had never been, and putting within their hearts that melody of love we have sung about this afternoon. Make them real Christians—not professors only, but possessors. May they know Thee Whom to know aright is life eternal. And knowing Thee may they be the means of introducing others to Thee, and to Thy love.

Oh, blessed Rose of Sharon, make Thyself as precious to them as Thou art to me. Fill these lives with the beauty and fragrance of Thy love, so that in that great final meeting before the Throne, all who are standing here may be found standing there, eternally joyous because their lives

WHY I AM A PREACHER 83

on earth were lived for Thee. This we ask in the Name which, to us, is the "sweetest note in seraph's song, sweetest name on mortal tongue— Jesus, blessed Jesus." Amen.

Let us all rise. Time does not permit our prolonging this service, but I want to ask you New York people, you, too, have given your hearts to Jesus today, to remember in your prayers our future campaigns in other cities. Will you? Thank you. I will not forget you either, and when I come back to New York some day, I hope I shall find all of you "growing in grace and in the knowledge of God our Lord and Saviour Jesus Christ."

I will ask Dr. Straton to pronounce the Benediction, then the choir will sing, *God Be With You 'Til We Meet Again*, as we go to our homes.

(Dr. Straton: *"Now unto Him that is able to keep you from falling, and to present you faultless before the presence of His glory with exceeding joy. To the only wise God our Saviour, be glory and majesty, dominion and power, both now and ever. Amen."*)

* * * *

I stand in silence beside my chair. There is a buzz of voices all around me. I'm glad no one is talking to me; I want to think. Did I do my best? Other things could have been included, too, no doubt. It's difficult to say everything one has in one's heart in so brief a time. But the Lord did help me. Praise His Name! And all those hundreds of hands lifted for prayer! And all those tears of penitence shed! Surely this has been a service in which the Lord has been "well pleased." It has been like getting saved all over again, this joy of seeing others raise their hands for prayer and confession of Jesus just as I did, five years ago.

Silently, fervently, I offer a prayer of thanksgiving to my Master. He has been so good to me; He has borne with me so many times when I was impatient and self-willed. In thankfulness for this wonderful service I feel I cannot but pledge allegiance always to His Gospel. So many people, today, have found Him precious unto their souls.

"Yes," I hear myself saying to the ushers, "I know I must go."

"We will take you through the crowd," they answer, and we are off, walking through a wide-swung door out into the street and into the waiting car. It is still raining; some of the people have no raincoats or umbrellas, yet they go smiling on their way. Surely being a Christian puts a permanent wave of happiness into one's life.

Here are Mother and Daddy, my little sister and cousin Gladys, all waiting for me! I am one of the family again; not a public speaker at all, but just a little girl of fourteen who is tremendously glad, even on a rainy day, like this, that she is a Christian—yes, and a preacher.

2. What Has Happened Since

The pages you have just read tell you the story of the memorable service held in Madison Square Garden, back in 1926. Since then, a number of things have happened.

I did not know then, of course, that in the following spring I should be back again in New York after having conducted revivals in Philadelphia and Norfolk and Chicago. In fact the campaign begun in Greater New York was continued from one place to another—beginning with fifteen days in Carnegie Hall, followed by a campaign in the old Claremont Rink, Brooklyn—since demolished but in which Moody and Sankey and Chapman and Alexander once held meetings. Then the Big Tent Cathedral, as it was known by thousands, was erected in the Bronx—near the Yankee Baseball Stadium—where five weeks of meetings were held.

These details appear to give the meetings an ordinary and stereotyped air, totally different from what they really were. Howard Wade Kimsey's remarkable solos and song-leading together with service rendered by the evangelistic choir helped to make these meetings spiritually successful and to crowd them with happy memories. Then there were the great prayer services held every evening preceding the larger meeting and attended by Protestants of all creeds as well as a large number of Catholics and Jews—these, too, are gratefully remembered.

In our office are hundreds of testimonies written by those who were brought to Christ or received some definite answer to prayer during the holding of these meetings. It was a time of great spiritual refreshing—as every revival should be—and the blessing of the Lord was given to speaker as well as listener, to those on the platform, as to those in the congregation.

Next came the Pittsburgh campaign, then the one conducted in Cleveland, Ohio, and after a few days meetings held in different churches in and around New York City, the meetings on the Western Coast.

It seemed strange to be in the West again, after having been away so long. There was Salem and Eugene, Oregon, and this time up into the State of Washington also—in Bellingham.

Following that campaign a flying trip to Ocala, Florida, was made, where I spent several days with the music festival directed by Homer Rodeheaver. Then, after spending my sixteenth birthday in Miami, we returned to Tulsa, Oklahoma, for a second campaign held, this time, in the City Auditorium. Following these meetings, the little Okla-

BEGINNING TO PREACH AT THE AGE OF ELEVEN

WHY I AM A PREACHER 87

homa city of Checotah received the Gospel most gladly, and we were encouraged by the response accorded by the people.

The summer of 1928 was the time of the ten weeks' meetings in the "Tent Cathedral" at the entrance of Prospect Park, Brooklyn. In those meetings more than in any that had preceded them I was enabled to get acquainted with the New York people who have been so interested in each campaign conducted in the great metropolis. And who wouldn't have desired to get better acquainted with people who for over two years had stood by one's side to pray and sing and help along the work? When those ten weeks were over, there were probably more than ten thousand people who sincerely wished they were just beginning, and this number included the preacher herself!

Ever since the meetings in Miami, in 1925, the people in that city had been calling us back and in 1928 we were able to respond to their invitation and return. That was how I spent the vacation I sorely needed—driving down to Florida from New York by car. Probably some people would not count that a particularly enjoyable holiday; but to one like myself who enjoys sitting behind the wheel watching the country road run back under me, as new stretches of scenery open up with each turn of the road, there could have been nothing finer; nothing, moreover, which would

88 WHY I AM A PREACHER

have prepared me as thoroughly for the strenuous time ahead of me in the Miami revival. And it *was* a strenuous time, partly because of the whole nation's attention being focussed on the Presidential elections and partly because Miami was below par in many ways spiritual and otherwise. But the Lord was with us, and we rejoiced in the souls who were saved.

Looking back on the next year, 1929, it appears to be densely crowded—almost overexpanded with ceaseless activity. There was, for example, the St. Petersburg revival held in the Christian and Missionary Alliance Tabernacle, with several services in addition, conducted on the way to the next campaign at Baltimore, Maryland—a night service in the First Methodist Church, Jacksonville; a night in Savannah, Georgia; another in Florence, S. C., a third in Lamberton, N. C.

The United Brethren Church in Baltimore witnessed a real evangelistic effort, in which many were won for the Lord. Two services nightly were made necessary before the meetings closed. During the meetings, the people of this church helped me to celebrate my seventeenth birthday. It would be impossible for me to forget all the care and kindness they expended in making it a delightful occasion for me.

A return campaign in Pittsburgh followed, and because it was Passion Week services were held in a different church each evening, commemorating the events of each successive day in the last week of our Lord's earthly ministry. Beach View Presbyterian, First Primitive Methodist Church, Greenfield Presbyterian Church, and the Christian and Missionary Alliance, were the churches cooperating. Easter Day marked the opening of the campaign proper, which began in the Carnegie Music Hall, later being transferred to the Soldiers' and Sailors' Memorial Hall, which provided greater seating capacity.

Followed an eleven-day union church campaign in Fayetteville, West Virginia, to which succeeded one in Erie, Pennsylvania, the campaign being conducted from May 15 to June 15, in the Armory. Following these services came a series of tent meetings held in a tent erected on the same spot as the one used the previous summer in Brooklyn. This time the services were held under the auspices of the Evangelistic Committee of New York City, who planned that I should speak from June 23 to June 30, closing on the evening of the latter, which was the opening service of a series of special meetings conducted by Dr. G. Campbell Morgan.

It was real summer time by now, and the weather proved propitious during a tent meeting held in Astoria, Long Island, under the auspices of the National Christian Co-workers, whose headquarters are in New York City.

August 18 marked the opening of my first campaign in Canada. This was in Winnipeg, Manitoba. The meetings were held in the Amphitheatre, seating seventy-five hundred. After concluding six weeks' services, a brief visit was paid to Saskatoon, Saskatchewan, which allowed us to return to the United States by October 20, to begin a month's revival in La Salle Avenue Baptist Church, Chicago. The close of this campaign made possible a two weeks series of meetings in Joliet, Illinois, before the coming of Christmas.

That brought us right up to 1930, the first campaign being held in Chicago from January 26 to February 2, in the Thoburn Methodist Episcopal Church, of which Dr. John H. DeLacy is Pastor, and of which I am proud to be a member. A return trip was then made to Fayetteville, West Virginia, for eleven days' meetings, after which we returned to New York City for the next campaign. Friends in and around the city planned what resulted in a most delightful reception and celebration of my eighteenth birthday, and marking my sixth anniversary as a preacher. The following day, being my birthday, marked the opening of a two weeks' revival in Spencer Memorial Presbyterian Church, Brooklyn. On Sunday mornings radio addresses were given over the Columbia broadcasting system, under the auspices of the Evangelistic Committee of New York City. Noonday services were conducted in old John Street Church, New York City, the oldest

Methodist church in America, founded in 1774, and of which Dr. Francis B. Upham is now pastor. A series of meetings was also held in Hanson Place Baptist Church, Brooklyn, where Dr. Mark Wayne Williams is pastor.

In 1926, I had spoken at two services held in the Wharton Memorial Methodist Church, Philadelphia. It was a joy, therefore, to be there again this year for a three weeks' revival, in the church where Dr. John G. Wilson is still pastor.

A month's campaign was then conducted in the First Baptist Temple, Portsmouth, Ohio, followed by a two weeks' revival in Charleston, W. Va., under the auspices of the Union Mission. Between the Charleston, West Virginia and the Madisonville, Kentucky, meetings, the latter in the First Methodist Episcopal Church (South), some friends made it possible for me to visit Oberammergau and witness the Passion Play, which proved a source of great inspiration to me.

The four closing months of 1930 were spent in Philadelphia with campaigns held in churches of different denominations in different parts of the city: Germantown in St. Stephen's Methodist Episcopal Church; West Philadelphia under the auspices of the Parkside Church Association, seven churches uniting; then in the Tioga Methodist Episcopal at Eighteenth and Tioga Streets; with a campaign in Columbia Avenue Church concluding just before Christmas.

With the coming of the New Year, 1931, comes also the renewed privilege of declaring the everlasting Gospel.

It will be seen how quite impossible it would be for me to attempt to give in detail the story of the different revivals which have been conducted during seven years. Let this suffice: they have made possible the salvation of hundreds of souls, and the Lord, who keeps all records clear, will reveal in the great day of final assize their true worth and the extent of their influence and helpfulness.

Undoubtedly we are living in a time of great revival-need; if this be conceded then is it not high time to call upon the Lord until He send down from heaven the latter rain so needful for the ripening of the harvest? We are out on the field all the time, working in various campaigns; but we know that the results of our labours are more assured by the people praying for us more than by anything we ourselves may do. You, my dear Christian friends, are the sustaining influence on which we depend; you are the people who keep our work going by the power and potency of your prayers.

Here, then, at last, is the little volume so many have been asking for. In its pages I have striven to tell you why I am a preacher. Some day a more comprehensive may be issued; but for the present I have endeavoured to confine myself, briefly, to that which led to my conversion and

WHY I AM A PREACHER

call to the preaching of the Gospel. In closing, let me repeat this word:

The prayers of Christian men and women mean encouragement and help in carrying on of this work and more than that, no evangelical work means all that it can unless it is supported by the unselfish prayers of Christian men and women.

You will pray for me, will you not?—pray that, like Paul, "utterance may be given unto me, that I may open my mouth boldly, to make known the mystery of the gospel."

II

GOSPEL MESSAGES

As delivered by Uldine Utley in her own services. Stenographically reported by Gladys Campbell.

I

THE ROSE OF SHARON *

Into this cathedral of the air we come, O Lord, to worship Thee. It is as though eternity were the altar before which we bow and space the great organ upon which to voice our praise. Thou art the God of the Universe, but Thou art more—Thou art become our salvation and our joy. We praise Thee that our hearts can be temples of worship, too, and that we may rejoice in Thy abiding presence with us. Speak, then, to us, O Lord, that our faith may be strengthened, our hope brightened and our love enlarged. This we ask in Thy holy Name. Amen.

IT has been suggested to me that I speak to you on "The Rose of Sharon." I have consented because I can never refuse a request for this particular message; it holds a charm and blessing for me which none other has, in the entire Word of God.

Rose of Sharon! No doubt these three words mean so much to me chiefly because of my wonderful Vision of the Rose (*see page* 33). But there are other reasons, too, and these are found within the pages of the Bible itself. For the Bible is not at all silent on this subject although, because so few sermons are preached upon it and so few

---
* Delivered over radio-station CJHS, Saskatoon, Saskatchewan, Canada, September 29, 1929.

books written about it, we may be apt to think it unimportant. Indeed, we seldom hear anyone mention Jesus as the Rose of Sharon, yet the Bible reveals Him so.

True, He is the Good Shepherd, the Counsellor, the Guide, the Lamb of God, the Divine Teacher, the Bright and Morning Star, the "altogether lovely," yet He is more. He is the Rose of Sharon. The proof of this is found first in that figurative book called Song of Solomon, presenting Christ as the Bridegroom and His Church, the Bride. The second chapter of the book and the first verse discloses the Bridegroom's voice saying to His Bride, "I am the Rose of Sharon."

The day I discovered these words, my mind went immediately back to the vision given me some months before; and although I thought I could not possibly appreciate it more than I already had, yet I found that I *did* appreciate it even more and certainly understood it more clearly, after I had read of the Rose of Sharon in the Song of Solomon.

"I am the Rose of Sharon." If Jesus is represented as the Morning Star, the Sun of Righteousness and the Lily of the Valleys it is not at all strange that He is also the Rose of Sharon. Growing yonder on the plains of Sharon, a fragrant, beautiful flower, of sturdy stock and tender petal, Rose of Sharon! A stranger might pass it by, but certainly not anyone who knew its religious sig-

BISHOP EDWIN HOLT HUGHES AND ULDINE UTLEY

nificance or its contribution to the reverence and worship of mankind, through the ages of the world.

Look for a moment at the other Scriptures on the subject. We shall think and speak of them in their own vernacular. Here is the first: Isa. 53: 2, "He shall grow up before him as a tender plant and as a root out of a dry ground." The second Scripture pertains to the ground from which the plant should rise. Isa. 1: 29, 30, "For they shall be ashamed of the oaks which ye have desired, and ye shall be confounded for the gardens that ye have chosen. For ye shall be as an oak whose leaf fadeth, and as a garden that hath no water." The relation between these two Scriptures is unmistakable. The history of the Hebrew people, from the earliest times, was but the stage-setting for one of the greatest dramas in history, the life and death of the world's Redeemer.

God took that little nation and made it a mighty power until Israel was no longer content that God should be their King. They wanted a man as king, "like other nations." They laid out their "beautiful gardens" of prosperity and splendour. They were going to have their "strong oak" (and do not forget that as the Rose is the king of flowers as the oak is the king of trees). The prophet warned them, however, that the strong oak was to fade, and their garden was to become dry, with every flower wilted and trampled down. Then! Out of the dry ground was to come the root that should blossom and fill the earth with its fragrance. Out of the parched earth should spring a "tender plant," and its very tenderness was to make it stronger than the strongest oak, king of trees.

At the coming of the Tender Plant a great effort was made to have it uprooted and destroyed. Instead, hundreds of other little plants in Bethlehem were destroyed but the one Plant sought had disappeared and was not harmed. Years later rumour testified to the existence of a Plant in the garden at Nazareth and so powerful had it become that many had been healed by believing on it. There was healing, then, in this miracle Plant. As unpretentious as their own Rose of the Sharon plains, it still held some strange, exotic fragrance which drove disease from tormented bodies and sorrow and bitterness from troubled hearts. From some strange plants we often get an ointment that soothes and heals and thus becomes a benefit to mankind, yet the plant itself derives its strength and life from the penetrating rays of the sun. Now the Scripture insists that Jesus is the "Sun of Righteousness arisen with healing in His wings." Is it no wonder then that being also the Rose of Sharon there should be in the virtue of His own name that inherent healing power which needs no assistance other than His own Words? We read that His "name is an ointment poured forth"—a healing, comforting, restoring nard.

The Rose of Sharon meant healing for the nations and salvation for the lost souls of mankind.

So, on this wise was the Rose of Sharon manifest. Root out of a dry ground, and the dry ground a result of Israel's desire for "the strong oak" and the "beautiful gardens." A time of dearth for the Jewish people, both politically and spiritually. Yet when spiritual conditions were such as to discourage even the most bold of those who still foretold the coming of the Messiah, He did come!

Simeon in the temple was told that he should not see death until he had seen the Lord's Christ. When Jesus was brought by His parents to the temple, Simeon lifted the Child in his arms, and we read that he took "him up in his arms, and blessed God, and said, Lord, now lettest thou thy servant depart in peace, according to thy word: For mine eyes have seen thy salvation." This was the witness to Simeon that the Messiah to come had already come, that salvation, such a precious gift, was already given for the birth of Jesus was a sure knowledge of salvation suffered for and provided, so dependable were the promises of God.

The Rose of Sharon, root out of a dry ground, as the world saw it, was growing up before God as a tender plant and remaining so in His sight forever.

"Lo, the world is gone after Him" was the statement made by some very troubled, and we might add, troublesome, Pharisees upon the Lord's entrance into Jerusalem. But despite their prejudice and ill-justice in many matters they, for once, had told the truth. The world was certainly gone after Him. There were Greeks there and they said to Philip, "Sir, we would see Jesus." It was the first voice from the outside world, the Gentile world was interested in the Messiah of the Jew. And history was to show that when the Jew had refused the message the apostles would say, "Lo, we turn to the Gentiles" and that salvation, which the angels said should be "Good tidings of great joy unto all people," were to be heard by the Gentile world as well as the Jew.

Jesus understood that, for when the Greeks were brought to Him it was as though He had looked down through the years to come and had seen the army of the Redeemed extend beyond the borders of His native land and into the kingdom of Rome and from thence throughout the earth. It was then He spoke of His death. It seemed strange to His disciples at the time but later they must have realized that, being the Rose of Sharon, His death must be following such a time of triumph.

It was, indeed. Palm leaves waved from hands lifted high, songs flung onto the breeze by voices hilarious with a kind of spiritual exhilaration: the multitudes which crowded the streets of the city and welcomed the Master seemed to believe Him more than a prophet. They accepted Him as the King's Son. In a few hours He was to die. He told them so amidst the palm leaves and the songs.

His death was like the splendour of a rose unexpectedly shattered and left with crimson petals scattered upon the walk. That is, unexpected to the passer-by, but not unexpected to the rose. One hour in its supreme glory, all its petals open to the sunshine, its fragrance wafted on the breeze—then, a little later, crushed and scattered. Dead.

That was the death of the Rose of Sharon. Crimson drops at the foot of the Cross told of the tragedy of the dying Rose. And it seemed so uncalled for, so without cause. Yet it had happened. No protest from the Rose. Simply submission to death—and through that submission, conquering it forever.

The disciples realized that afterward. It had not been useless and vain as first it had seemed. His death was the greatest contribution ever made to the life of the world, for this was a miracle Rose. After its shattered petals had fallen they were gathered again into the full-blown perfection which had been its beauty before. The Rose alive again! Risen with a splendour with which even its former ministry had not enhanced it!

The Rose of Sharon still lives. Here is the miracle, that after two thousand years we still feel and know the presence and glory of His own Divine personality. He is still real, still precious, still abiding, still gracious. "Jesus Christ the same yesterday and today and forever."

Now, before this little instrument I need only to whisper the words, "Jesus, Rose of Sharon," and my voice is carried to you who are now listening, living miles away from where I now stand, yet there where you are you say in return, "Amen," and know that what I say is true: He still lives, His beauty and fragrance still permeates the world and you open your heart wider today that it may be suffused with this eternal sweetness from the Rose of Sharon.

Nor do we omit that Scripture which refers to His earthly reign. I read from Isaiah 35: "The wilderness and the solitary place shall be glad for them; and the desert shall rejoice, and blossom as the rose, It shall blossom abundantly, and rejoice even with joy and singing: the glory of Lebanon shall be given unto it, the excellency of Carmel and Sharon, they shall see the glory of the Lord, and the excellency of our God."

At His first coming He was the tender Plant, Root out of a dry ground. When He returns the whole earth will be filled with His glory and never did Rose have such a conspicuous part as will then be had by our blessed Rose of Sharon.

We have mentioned four specific Scriptures relative to the subject of Rose of Sharon yet it seems to me, as I turn the pages of the Bible, that every verse pertaining to the attributes or ministry of Jesus makes more clear to us this picture of Him.

Tarry a moment longer. Let us think again of that first Scripture mentioned: "I am the Rose of Sharon." The Bridegroom speaking to His Bride is seeming to say, "Do I mean something more to you than a provider? Do you love me more for what I am *to* you than for what I do *for* you?" He portrays Himself here as the source of all joy and delight, of all beauty and fragrance to the Bride. The rose is not valuable for its usefulness. All the value there is to a rose is the pleasure it brings to those who look upon it. Jesus would have us "delight ourselves also in Him," would have us spend time in His presence not to pray for things but to worship and adore Him. It is thus that we gain something of His own Spirit, its lowliness and its loftiness, its submission and its triumph, its silence and it eloquence.

When His Spirit dwells in your heart richly, by faith, and you show by your daily life that you love Christ, it will be because in those secret moments of worship and adoration, the fragrance and beauty of the Rose of Sharon filled your heart and thus sent its radiance forth into every department of your life.

2

THE RIGHT OF WAY *

We praise Thee, tonight, dear Lord God, that Thou didst really prepare the way. We cannot fully understand how salvation could come to us, but Thou didst find the way. Thou didst send the great and mighty Saviour and it is by His Name, we enter Thy presence tonight.

In His name we open this precious Bible and ask that Thou shalt give us His Words of life. O, speak Thou tonight, because we want to listen, we want to obey; grant that the same love which has shown us the way may be shown the unsaved, that they, too, may find peace in Jesus and by accepting and believing His Gospel may they enter into the kingdom through the gate of repentance. For the glory of His Name we ask it. Amen.

IN my hand I hold a little green book, on the front cover of which are these words: "Traffic Ordinance, 4576." It tells us just which vehicles have the right of way, and just what rules must be obeyed, and tells us about the traffic laws for the city of Bellingham. I don't even need to read it to you, for most of you have copies. But have you ever thought of how the Lord sends out His vehicles and they should have the right of way?

---

* Delivered in Bellingham, Washington, February 14, 1928.

(Above) SPEAKING TO SAILORS ABOARD THE U.S.S. *PENNSYLVANIA*
(Below) MEETING IN WALL STREET, NEW YORK CITY

The Lord has many vehicles to carry on His work. We read in Jeremiah of how the prophet was badly discouraged because the people gave no heed to his message and very much disheartened because they made fun of him, and this is what he said: "I will not make mention of him"—he was speaking of the Lord—"not speak any more in his name." And then, what happened to that prophet? He himself records it: "But his word was in mine heart as a burning fire shut up in my bones," he says, "and I was weary with forbearing, and I could not stay." And the Lord blessed the word he spoke because he no longer made objections or excuses.

Oh, I wish that God would set sirens calling, and whistles blowing and arrest people—not to put them into jail, but to bring them to repentance! Some people think it is a sign of weakness to put up a cry to the Lord for help; yet these same people would not hesitate to call for an ambulance in the event of an accident. It is certainly much better to enter an ambulance and get saved, than to stay outside and die.

In this booklet we read about lights, turns—right and left hand turns—ambulances, fire-wagons, and also about city repair vehicles. I don't doubt but that these are good rules, and that in obeying them the city has a good system of traffic control. But, for all that, I know the Lord could make Bellingham a whole lot better than it is at present if only its citizens would pay a little attention to God's rules.

If we hinder God from working we cannot get His blessing. He must have the right of way, full sway, in our lives. Back in history we see that the people who accomplished something for His glory were those who were "crucified with Christ," whose old selfish nature was mortified, and who had "the life also of Jesus" manifest in their mortal flesh.

And that brings to mind what is said in John 7: 17—that if you want to do God's will He will *show* you His will. "If any man will do His will, he shall know of the doctrine, whether it be of God, or whether I speak of myself." If you want to obey the laws of this city, get this little green book and read about them. You will learn what you should do and what you should not do. Similarly, if you want to do God's will, get the dear old Book we call the Bible and read what He wants you to do! Oh, the Lord must have His right of way, and He will make that way plain as He has promised: "If any man will to do his will, he shall know of the doctrine."

If you are to succeed in doing His will, your heart must be in what you do, for we read we must serve Him "not with eyeservice, as men-pleasers; but as servants of Christ, doing the will of God from the heart." That is the only place from which we can do God's will—from the heart; and if you are going to do God's will you will have to ask Him to speak to your heart by the power of His Holy Spirit; then you must put forth the effort needed, to fulfill His will, according to the revelation He has given you. By hesitating to do this many lose all the joy of Christian living. The right of way! God must have it, if He is to do anything with your life in this present world.

Once, in the history of the race, God had the right of way and the result was that everything was very beautiful. But it was not for long; for Satan, who was God's enemy before the day of creation, was careful to interfere, to come to the Garden of Eden with his lies. He told Adam and Eve they would become wise and mighty as gods, if only they would disobey God. "Thou shalt not die," he assured them; so, even though the Lord had told them differently, Adam and Eve thought that the Serpent was right.

They did not do as the Lord told them, but believed Satan's lies instead, and were turned out from the Garden. Today Satan is still whispering, "God hath *not* said," and if we do not "will to do His will," if we are not giving Him complete right of way in our lives, we shall be giving Satan the right of way, and doing Satan's will.

In the eighth chapter of Romans we read—"For they that are after the flesh do mind the things of the flesh; but they that are after the Spirit the things of the Spirit. For to be carnally minded is death; but to be spiritually minded is life and peace. Because the carnal mind is enmity against God: for it is not subject to the law of God, neither indeed can be. So then *they that are in the flesh cannot please God.*"

To be spiritually minded! That is a very high standard! Some people, standing on tip-toe, even, can barely reach it. But we do not have to stand on tip-toe, we do not have to struggle and fret and try. The Holy Spirit will come into our lives and help us, if we so desire.

Satan came to Eden and the hearts of our first parents were turned against God. The earth was no longer the happy place it had been when all was in God's will, but seemed to turn to chaos and confusion. God did not want it to be this way but Adam and Eve had made it so; thus they were separated from Him, by a great gulf.

God is a great God of purity and holiness, the Creator of heaven and earth by the Word of His power, and an infinite God whose ways our finite minds cannot grasp. Adam and Eve had gone away from Him when they opened their minds to what Satan had said, when he told them they "should be as gods." In other words, man wanted the right of way and when he got it he found that the whole way before him was congested because God had planned the way and the mind of man was not adapted to running the universe, or even to the management of his own little part of it.

The hand of God had to be back of it all and when man took the right of way all was confusion. That is why, when the race makes progress in one way it is liable to retard in another—to gain ground in science and commerce and education and to lose out religiously.

Yet, something happened two thousand years ago, that just seemed to change everything! God promised His Son should redeem all mankind. He opened a new way, and while the old way was filled with sin and sorrow and darkness, love came in, and

"Love found a way to redeem my soul,
 Love found a way that could make me whole;
 Love found a way to the cross of shame,
   Love found a way—O praise his Holy Name!"

Indeed, our hearts are filled with praises because He opened up a new way of which we read in the tenth chapter of Hebrews: "Having therefore, brethren, boldness to enter into the holiest by the blood of Jesus, By a new and living way, which he hath consecrated for us, through the veil, that is to say, his flesh."

Christ died for us, and in giving His life in human flesh for our redemption, He opened the way of salvation, and through it, to eternal life. The only way by which we are able to come into the very presence of God, today, is by the atonement Jesus made for us through His death.

Man needed a guide, one to show him the way, and that is why, when he had the right of way, everything was confusion. He had certain laws, certain ritual which appealed to his mind but his heart was not touched. But when Jesus came He didn't appeal to the mind alone, or to the carnal side of man, but to the heart and spiritual side of him. He died for us, gave His life for us, and when He rose again on the third day, from the dead, conquered Satan.

"He is dead—see, I have stopped the beating of His heart," said Satan. Yet, on the third morning the grave opened, and Jesus stood there, alive! And where were the boasts of Satan and his hosts?

If, today, you mention that Jesus died for our salvation, the devil will try to prove that He didn't, for he is against the message of Jesus. Why? Because Jesus conquered him. "Forasmuch then as the children are partakers of flesh and blood, he also himself likewise took part of the same; that through death he might destroy him that had the power of death, that is, the devil; And deliver them who through fear of death were all their life-time subject to bondage."

"Jesus isn't real, salvation isn't real," he still tries to tell people. It is through his slaves—poor, unregenerate sinners—that Satan still tries to say, "Don't believe the Bible. Don't believe that salvation is real." That is why he is so enraged at the thought of someone serving Jesus when that one has found the Way. He has lost one of his prisoners! His hold has been loosened on a soul!

Yet, when Jesus comes into the heart of any who have found Him, He brings with Him such joy that immediately all Satan's lies and threatenings are powerless. "If the Son therefore shall make you free, ye shall be free indeed." Yet to maintain that freedom the newly-converted must let Jesus have the right of way in their individual lives; they must let Him speak through their actions, their words, their every task and every pleasure.

By this means, which operates unconsciously because it springs from a heart-experience, they are able to win others, and those who are thus won to bring still others until the number swells and Christ is "Lord of all."

Only today I was thinking of a story, which was in our second readers at school. I believe it was a conversation carried on by the sun and wind, a dispute over which could make a certain man first take off his coat. The man walked down the road, all unsuspecting. The wind said he could accomplish the feat more quickly than the sun. "I can make him take it off the more quickly," said the sun.

So the wind began to blow. It blew and blew and as it grew colder the man drew his coat the more closely. All the while the sun was smiling the wind was puffing out his cheeks to the full and sending fierce blasts of chilling cold towards the walking man; but he just turned up his collar, buttoned his coat snugly, and said, "This is certainly a windy day."

When the wind gave up the task the sun began to shine and glow. All was still along the road. Presently, it grew warm, so warm that it was no longer comfortable for the man to keep his coat on—so off came the coat!

Why was the wind defeated if it were not because he took a "cold" and negative position in compelling the man to do his will?

Satan is the taskmaster Jesus talked about. Even after a person is converted the devil tries to compel him to do as he says. "I will get the right of way in your life," he says to the Christian. And what happens? The Christian just buttons up his coat that much tighter, and trusts the Lord to take care of him, because the Sun of Righteousness has the right of way! The love of Jesus, like the warm health-giving ray of the sun, floods down upon us and our cloak of prejudices and selfish plans come off!

Jesus has won the heart of the world through love, and He not only persuaded man to do His will but gave him the desire of heart to do His will. "The preparations of the heart in man, and the answer of the tongue, is from the Lord." (Prov. 16:1.) He blesses us so, and in such abundance—the precious Rose of Sharon is not sparing in fragrance and beauty—we cannot find it in our hearts to do anything else but adore and obey.

This is God's plan. Man was lost and undone; his heart was hardened; he was unhappy because he had not found reality and wondered if there were a Great Sovereign Will ruling the world? Then Jesus came and died and showed His great power by rising again, sending out His followers that they might preach and tell the people of His death, of His power to *save*, and His power to *keep* those who would follow Him and say, "Not my will but Thine be done." In the experience of tens of thousands He has found what He can do, when given the right of way. That is to say, without preamble or reservation, we do exactly what the Lord tells us to do—no more and no less!

It is so simple. We have only to believe, to repent of our sins, to love Him and serve Him with all our hearts. Believing is the chief factor in our being saved, and obedience the chief factor in our being *kept* saved. We believe that "Christ Jesus came into the world to save sinners": that is the past tense of believing. We also believe, "He is the rewarder of them that diligently seek Him," and that is the present tense. He rewards me *now*. That is active faith. To believe in the past tense, and in the present, is to give Christ the right of way, both in the mind (accepting the fact of His death) and in the heart (accepting salvation as a free gift). We know that "as many as received him, to them gave he power to become the sons of God, even to them that believe on his name; Which were born, not of blood, nor of the will of the flesh, nor of the will of man, but of God." To receive Christ is to receive His Word and by that His will. Thus we have power to live the life of a real Christian.

"I delight to do thy will, O my God," the Psalmist said. If David were still alive I am sure that, after all these centuries, he would repeat his words. There is not a thing that God plans for our lives that is not to our joy or profit. We cannot understand, even though we look back on all the ages that are gone, all this plan means; but God understands. He has been working it out, day by day, age by age. What a happy day it will be when we can stand before Him and know that His plan was carried out throughout our earthly life; that, by the accepting of His free grace, we have measured up to His expectation of us; that, because we have been "kept in the love of God," we have never disappointed Him!

One of the greatest men God ever enlisted in His service was a man who had to learn, by virtue of humiliation and defeat, the meaning of the will of God. He was a popular rabbi. His following being great, and his will being strong, he did just about whatever he set his mind and hands to do.

He had tremendous influence, because he believed with all his heart what he believed, and did what he did with all his strength. He did not believe in Christianity. Christians—and most of them were the poor and the untutored—were fanatics and dangerous to the ancient Jewish faith. Whoso was the enemy of these heretics would be a friend of God. To rid the world of these people was to do a deed of goodness immeasurable.

On his way, with orders to put the Christians to death, this man, Saul of Tarsus, met another Man, Jesus of Nazareth. Saul was humiliated, smitten to the earth by the blinding light of the Divine Presence. Even his men who were with him marvelled, for "hearing a voice they saw no man."

"Who art thou, Lord?" Saul asked in fear and apprehension. "Who is the cause of all this? My purposes are destroyed, the strong conviction I have entertained topples and falls, my will wavers, Who art thou, Lord?" Back came the answer, given with all the charm known to those who had heard the matchless voice by Galilee: "I am Jesus."

That settled it; Jesus had won! In that moment Saul repented, and his wilfulness and presumption vanished. He had taken for granted that God's will was his own, but now he discovered that Jesus was the guide, that He alone could clearly indicate the will of God. After all, Jesus had said, "I come not to destroy the law but to fulfil." Thus Saul was not needed to defend the ancient law: rather was he needed to strengthen the fulfilment of the law which completed and glorified it.

Here is the record of Saul's absolute surrender: "Lord, what wilt thou have me to do?" That was acknowledging Jesus Lord—giving Him the right of way. It has been rightly said, that "a man is a fool who still wants to take charge of his life after he had discovered a great God."

Saul may have been wilful, proud and presumptuous, but he was no fool. He acknowledged Jesus as Lord. He asked only to be allowed to do His will. He was told to go to Damascus where "it shall be told thee what thou shalt do."

Thus he began to walk by faith. Blinded because of the light that had smitten him to the earth, he had to be led into the city. Through the city gates he passed into an entirely new life, a life so utterly different from the old that his entire will was submerged into the will of God, through Christ. He was no longer Saul of the old will and way but Paul of the new; no longer a persecutor but an Apostle.

Through suffering, sacrifice, strenuous journeyings, constant ministering to the needy; bearing his cross, declaring his Gospel, serving his Christ, he went on; never faltering, never failing; "true to the heavenly vision," he "counted all things loss that he might win Christ." He won the favour and blessing of Christ because he lost his own wilfulness and selfishness.

It was best for Paul that he let God have "right of way," and it is best for you. Do the wise thing, the thing which, after an eternity is past, you will still be glad that you did.

Let God take charge. You don't even need to see the blue print He has made for your life. "The just shall live by faith." Do that which you feel to be the will of God for you today, and, tomorrow, the way will be even brighter, for, "the path of the just is as shining light, that shineth more and more unto the perfect day." The paramount question is: Have you found the path? Are you on the way? If you hold nothing back, offer no excuse, yield wholly and utterly to Christ you can confidently answer "Yes!"

3

THE CHRIST OF THE MASSES *

Blessed Master, we stand in Thy presence, because we are needy. Certainly the multitudes—those who thronged Thee when Thou wast here on the earth—were not more needy than we. Certainly their hunger for righteousness was not more keen than ours. Certainly their desire to know about Thee and to hear Thy words was no greater than ours is today. We stand just now in Thy presence and ask that as we read Thy Word and talk about it and listen to it we may do so with great understanding and great reverence. And, O Master, as Thy Word is given today may it be food for the hungry, drink for the thirsty, healing for the wounded, comfort for the sorrowing, life to those who are dead in trespasses and in sins. We ask it in that Name, through which we expect an answer—the Name of Jesus. Amen.

WE have different ideas among us, today, as to just what kind of a life most glorifies God. There could be a debate on that subject, perhaps, yet there are certain things which seem definite to me (I speak, of course, out of my own interpretation). If our life glorifies God it is one that is patterned very closely indeed after the life of Jesus. Of His life

---

* Delivered in John Street Methodist Episcopal Church, New York City, March 18, 1930.

Above (Left) ON VACATION ABROAD. (Right) ULDINE AND OVELLA UTLEY IN DUTCH DRESS
Below (Left) CLOSE FRIENDS. (Right) "CAP'N CANARY," THE CAMPAIGN CAR

I might speak in one sentence: He talked with God and talked with man; He walked with God and walked with man; He communed with God and communed with man. There are some who believe that living a hermit's life is more to the glory of God's Name; yet, a marble statue, however flawless it may seem, and no matter how much admiration it may provoke, possesses no life, nor moves any one to speak. It may be life-like, but it cannot be life-giving.

So I say to you that the Christian life is not something to be admired and seen, but something that is human and practical; something tangible enough and audible enough to present a definite message, every day. That is something that a statue, no matter how beautiful and perfect, cannot do. There is an old legend that has been passed down from generation to generation. I cannot remember all its details, but in substance it deals with the desire of a monk to live in God's presence. He spent many hours, almost all day and night, in a little tower-room high above a great cathedral. After many days and weeks and months so spent, he cried out desperately to God and said, "Oh, that I might find God, where He is!" And we are told that a voice came distinctly to him, saying, "God is not up here, but down among the people who need Him in their daily lives. Go and seek Him *there!*"

We cannot know God and hold ourselves aloof

from the people. We cannot know Him and close the door between the Church and the multitude wanting to know God—close the door between the people and our lives and say, "I have no time for you, only for God." We read that "Jesus increased in wisdom and stature and favour with God and man," as though the record would tell us that He spent time not only with God, but with man. And that was very important. If Jesus had not mingled with the multitude, taught them patiently, with ever so much of long-suffering and gentleness, what would our idea of Him be? It would be something brief and exclusive. We would see Him in just a few instances only: We should see Him, for example, when baptized in the Jordan, as the Voice from heaven said, "This is my beloved Son in whom I am well pleased." We should see Him on the Mount of Transfiguration, when His face did shine as the sun and His garments were white as snow. We would see Him on Easter morn, alive, risen, glorified. But because He moved among the people we see Him in many other and blessed ways. We see Him as the sick come to Him for healing. We see Him as young and old come to Him with their problems. We see Him as little children are brought by their mothers that He might bless them. We see Him as He talks with His disciples. Sometimes the questions they asked Him seemed foolish and childish but the Lord was very patient. He answered their questions. There were times when they made comments which did not seem to be in any important relation to the all-important subject of saving souls; but the Lord counselled them and helped them. They strove with one another as to who would be on one side of Him and who on the other, but the Lord corrected their mistaken views, and He did it without laughing at their mistakes, at all.

What do we see, then? We see the human Christ, the Saviour-God, the God-man, the One who "was man as though He were never God and God as though never man." And it is this combination that is represented to us in the Scripture as the ideal for our Christian lives. "Pure religion and undefiled *before God* and the Father is this, *To visit* the fatherless and widows in their affliction, and to keep himself unspotted from the world."

Here it is: first, before God, next, to visit the fatherless. First, before God: communion with Him, blessed fellowship with Him; then a turning-about to help our fellows; to visit the sick and dying; to be willing to sacrifice and suffer (if need be) in order to do this. That is the work and walk of a Christian in the sight of God.

Our lives are unbalanced if we lack either of these obligations. If we live a life of unceasing prayer, of separation from all worldly interests, in the study of God's Word and in worship, that is all very well, and very necessary. But we must not be in touch with God and not in touch with man. What is the benefit to the world of all God has done for us unless we give out to others the news of what He means to us? Again: we must not have communion with worldly interests and no fellowship with God. Some do not walk with God, have no delight in the Scriptures, cannot say with the Psalmist, "On his law do I meditate day and night." Their minds are set on worldly things.

True enough is the axiom which declares that "water does not rise above its source"; in like manner, one cannot have the power to lift those with whom he associates every day unless he have this life in God. So it becomes a problem, this of living with God and for God, simply because it is not only a life of communion *with* God, but also that of working *for* God.

Dwight L. Moody once said that you can work without praying but you can never pray without working, and I wonder if that isn't so? For certain it is that we can have many plans and endeavour together with great egotism to carry them out ourselves, without Divine help and guidance; but when we come into the presence of God and get a vision of eternal values, we want to work. It gives us an ambition for new and prayerful service.

So, I say it is not the life entirely hidden from

the world that is of value, for it is selfish to receive a blessing from God and not want to be a blessing to others. To pride ourselves in being "holier than thou," or to boast that we "have more religion than Mr. Brown," is not a thing we should work for. We should desire to be so humble and patient that those about us will say, "That man has been with Jesus. I think of Jesus when I talk with him." Unsaved people have been known to say of some Christians: "They know more about the Lord, they know more about the Bible, than I do. Somehow, their life is higher than mine. They accomplish more than I seem to accomplish. They have a greater idea of the importance of little things in daily life than I." Do they speak that way of you?

Jesus lifted up His eyes and saw the people. He was in the midst of them. It is in the midst of the people that the most work can be done for Jesus. "Where two or three are gathered in my name, there am I." On the mountain we have fellowship with God; but we do not build "three tabernacles upon the mount" and there abide. Instead, we must come down again into the valley. It was upon the mountain top Elijah went when he prayed for rain. He told his servant to look at the sky, but he returned saying he saw no sign. "Look again!" commanded the prophet. "Hasten and look. There must be a cloud even the size of a man's hand." And there was! A great shower came down, after a long period of drought and famine, and it was because Elijah was in God's presence, on the mountain-top. But see him again, this time down under the juniper tree. "O, Lord, let me die," he cried. He had come down from the mountain-top and left his experience behind him. He was so discouraged, that he felt it was no use, anyway. It were better that he should die. The Lord's prophets before him had been slain, he would not be the first; besides, he was about the only one left who had remained true to Jehovah-God. The more he thought about this, himself, the more dismayed and troubled he became. In such a state of mind, Elijah could do nothing to help others.

I take another example: Once there was One on the mountain-top, whose face did shine as the sun, whose garments were so white that we are told no fuller on earth could whiten them. And then He came down, but He brought His experience with Him. We are told in Mark's Gospel that a father, "one of the multitude," came to Him (Jesus was there, in the multitude) and brought with him his sick child. He said, "Lord, I believe; help thou mine unbelief." And Jesus cast out the evil spirit and healed the child.

Jesus had come down from the mountain-top and brought His experience with Him to the valley. The mountain blessing He received He took to the people in the valley. Don't leave your experience on the mountain-peak. Take it to the world. Do not be afraid to walk down the crowded streets. You have the Lord ever before you, for God walks with you alone on the mountain-top, and He walks with you in the valley, as you walk with others. No loneliness can bar God out, and no place can be too crowded to allow fellowship with God, if you desire it.

You are absent-minded if you do not walk with God. "Thou wilt keep him in perfect peace, whose mind is stayed on thee: because he trusteth in thee." The Lord *will* keep you in perfect peace, but your *mind* must be stayed upon Him, even as your feet are upon the earth. Jesus had times of solitude as well as times of sociability—times when He was alone in prayer—you must have them or you will have no power in your life—times when He was in the midst of the people. Unless you spend time with God you will not have the spiritual power with people. If you spend all your time with people you will not do them any good; but if you spend time with God, you will do them all sorts of good. If you have power with God, you will have power with man.

If you are drawn to the Lord others will be influenced, too. They will take notice that you have been with Jesus. The multitude came to Jesus. He was so patient. And I tell you we must have time with the Lord or we shall be impatient.

Jesus had great understanding. You hear

people say, "Oh, you may like that one, but if you knew him as well as I do, you wouldn't like him so much." They are wrong. It is not that we know them too well, but that we don't know them well enough.

The Lord is able to understand, because His knowledge of us is thorough. Our knowledge is not. We cannot reach the cause of things. He can. Our opinions and judgments are limited to our faulty comprehension. We have difficulty even in understanding ourselves. Christ has none. He shows us what is the matter with us in an instant's time when we have spent hours thinking in vain. He does not excuse sin, He frees us from it. But He frees us through truth—and that truth is His own thorough knowledge.

He can see in one that you may despise, the making of a great messenger of the Word, one possessing sterling character. The piece of gold may have fallen in the tar, but the Lord knows how to get the tar off. It may appear to be covered up, but Jesus, who fully understands, can, by seeing our good points and bringing them to the light, decrease those things which hinder, and through decreasing them finally banish them altogether.

Rest assured that if you spend a lot of time with the Lord, you will be able, finally, to see things a little more as the Lord sees them. You will begin to look through God's eyes, for God saw, "and behold, everything was good." Through bringing out the good things, He decreases those that are evil and unprofitable.

Jesus lifted up His eyes, and saw the people, and when He saw them He had compassion on them. You remember the parable of the Good Samaritan. When the wounded traveller was lying by the roadside, bleeding and half-dead, one passed him by without acknowledging that he saw the man's need. And another came and saw him, but passed by. Then the last man came where he was, "and when he saw him, he had compassion on him. And went to him, and bound up his wounds, pouring in oil and wine, and set him on his own beast and brought him to an inn, and took care of him."

The first two men in the parable represent us when we are without any enlightenment regarding the importance of things in the Lord's sight. The first man didn't want to acknowledge there was any need. But when Jesus looked and saw the multitude He had compassion. The second man came and looked at the traveller's need. He was sorry for the poor fellow but that was all. First, if we do not see the world's plight and its need of the Gospel we shall not be anxious to bring them the Gospel. Then, even when we have come to the place of seeing the world's need we must have love in our hearts—the love the Scripture teaches—to enable us not only to see the need but to meet it.

Jesus lifted up His eyes and saw the people and when He saw them He had compassion. His compassion was manifest. He did something for them. We are told He helped them. I want you to notice the different instances where He had compassion. And, never forget, this compassion is manifest only in the two-fold life: time with God and time with man. One, in Matthew's version, runs as follows: "But when he saw the multitudes, he was moved with compassion on them, because they fainted, and were scattered abroad, as sheep having no shepherd."

He saw all this great crowd. Understand, He knew them, everyone. With a capacity which was His alone, as the Creator of heaven and earth, as the great I AM, as the First and the Last. He knew them as individuals as well as He did as a multitude, and when He saw them He had compassion because they fainted. He says: "Come unto Me, all ye that labour and are heavy-laden, and I will give you rest." They fainted, they were in need of rest, and He offered them rest.

The compassion of Jesus is a wonderful thing. In New York City the people need rest. They are worried and their nerves are on edge. They rush here and there, and many rise from their beds in the morning wishing for just a big expanse of sky, just a time of thought and rest by some cool stream, just a little peace and quiet. Yet, Jesus is able to give rest to this great city, or in any time of need. He is able to lead beside still waters, and into green pastures. No matter the rush and noise and the cares of the day, He spreads over us the great sky, and smiles upon us. He has compassion, and it is so marvellous and such a practical compassion that it supplies our needs. In the fourteenth chapter of Matthew's Gospel we are told that "Jesus went forth, and saw a great multitude, and was moved with compassion toward them, and he healed their sick." They were in such need of healing, and Jesus healed them. Oh, Jesus is still the greatest of all physicians! There is no hand so calm, so sure, and so absolutely dependable as that of Jesus. He never misses a mark. He never makes a mistake. Anywhere, everywhere, He is the Great Physician and His healing results from His compassion and understanding of our needs.

Again: Matthew tells us that Jesus said, "I have compassion on the multitude, because they continue with me now three days, and have nothing to eat." That was the reason. The disciples realized they didn't need any other reason. They did not need Jesus to say, "You must get busy." His reason was, "I have compassion." He did not have to say, "They need food and I must get them food." He simply said they needed it, which meant that He would give it to them. Why do we repeat with such confidence day after day, "Give us this day our daily bread"? Is it not that we realize that the Lord has an interest in the material side of our lives—in the spiritual and the material also?

There were those blind men. Tapping with their sticks on the cobblestones they made out the general direction of the crowd, stumbling along, determined to locate Jesus, the One Who healed. Then, Jesus saw them, and when He saw them He had compassion upon them, and "touched their eyes and immediately their eyes received sight, and they followed him." No wonder they did! They had stumbled along so long. Sometimes they stopped with a start against a stone wall. And people had said, "Get out of the way! Why are you in the way?" But they heard the voice of Jesus and came asking for healing, and He had compassion upon them. He reached out His hand —that wonderful, healing hand—and touched their closed eyes, and they were opened and the men saw Jesus!

You see He had compassion upon them—such great compassion that He did something. You have no compassion upon the unsaved of New York City unless you do something to save them —unless you go to where the needy are and help them.

Jesus had compassion. The men saw Jesus and

when they saw Him they followed Him. It was His compassionate love that drew them, and in the following they learned to love others as He had loved them.

Again we are told (first chapter of Mark, verse 41), that Jesus had compassion upon the leper. Other people pitied him, but Jesus was different, He reached out and touched him. There was compassion in that touch, but there was also power. Power to heal, because God had given it to Him.

The seventh chapter of Luke tells us that Jesus' compassion took the form of comfort and joy. There was a funeral procession. A mother, dressed in mourning, walked beside the bier of her son. Jesus stopped—you can see the picture—and said, "Weep not." He didn't want sadness. He didn't want the blackness of death. He wanted life and joy and gladness. But His compassion did not just let Him say a few comforting words. He raised the boy from the dead.

Jesus fully understands your sorrow. He fully understands need. If you go back to our text you will see that when Jesus lifted up His eyes He had compassion. Then He began to teach the people many things. The Lord has compassion upon New York City, and He would like to teach they that dwell therein.

We think we know a lot; but there are still some things we need to be taught. Some of these only faith and God can teach us, and we need to know them. With the humility of a little child, we must come to the Lord for a lesson, to hear His words, to listen to what He has to say, to see what the world cannot help us see.

You would live a Christian life? Then live it among the people, who need to be shown what kind of a life can be lived for Christ. Do not hold yourself aloof and say, "I must live my life alone." You are in this world to be something more than a "marble-statue Christian." You are to be a life lived, a voice speaking for Christ, every day.

Have you compassion upon the multitude? The Lord has compassion upon you. He seeks to understand you, and succeeds. You may not have complete success in understanding your fellows but, at least you can try, and the more time you spend with God, the more you will understand. He knows your problems. He asks you to enter into fellowship with Him and have compassion upon the multitude.

As Jesus loves you, so, also, ought you to love and, if need be, "lay down your life for the brethren." So it means the possession of practical ideals; it means that your life must be lived, first, for God, and next, in the busy haunts of men. Bring the glory you have received from Him, into use, in your life among men. Bring your mountain-top experience down into the valley. This is what Jesus did, and a servant is never greater than his Lord.

4
ADRIFT *

Blessed Lord, we realize it is so very easy to drift without the feeling of Thy hand ever in our own; without the knowledge that Thou art ever beside us; without the voice of Thy promises to encourage us it is so easy to drift! Lord, so many times we have failed to walk with Thee and talk with Thee, and hold counsel with Thee; as a result many of us are without the joy of Thy constant fellowship, without the knowledge that our hearts are really right with Thee. We pray, Lord, that those who are drifting may be helped to head their boats upstream and not drift along carelessly with the current. May the Holy Spirit show us what we ought to do and help us to start doing it. Direct us in the right way. We ask it in the precious Name to which we ascribe all honour and glory. Amen.

IN the first and second verses of the second chapter of Hebrews, the sacred writer presents his argument for holy living: because of the greatness of God, because of the love of God, because of the manifestation of His power, because of the Gospel which Jesus Himself delivered into the hands of His apostles, and which the apostles not only put on the written scroll, but, by word of mouth, handed down to us. For this reason we are told to give "the more earnest heed

---
* Message delivered, Sunday afternoon, July 15, 1928, in the "Tent Cathedral," Brooklyn, N. Y.

to the things which we have heard, *lest at any time we should let them slip.*"

It is a comparatively easy matter to be fully consecrated to the Lord and intent on living the Christian life, and, then almost unconsciously to begin to slip back into the old way of living. Jesus must have thought of that when He said, "Strive to enter in." When we cease striving we cease progressing. Our text emphasizes this truth: it is possible for one to receive the Gospel, be touched and even transformed by its message, and then through carelessness and neglect turn a dissenting ear to it and lose that life-giving portion and blessing that was his. All lost, just by allowing it to carelessly slip away.

The process is just like a boat in the middle of the stream which slips away and drifts out and down because there is no one watching to keep it in the right course. There are those in the Christian Church who, after being saved, neglect this "great salvation" which should be "worked out" in their daily lives. They go the effortless way of the current.

The message of this passage in Hebrews, then, is that we are not to let these opportunities slip by. In the first chapter of this book we see all that God did. It reviews His work, His power, His greatness. "God, who at sundry times and in divers manners spake in time past unto the fathers by the prophets," it tells us. Then the Son came and the

A THRONGED GATHERING IN PHILADELPHIA

angels, and then the ministers. And to them all we are told to give earnest heed. We recall the time when we knelt at the foot of the Cross and gave our all to Jesus, when we felt our sins blotted out and when we knew our names were written in heaven, just as clearly as if we saw them with our mortal eyes. We remember how we said with gladness, "I know in whom I have believed," and felt our whole lives filled with music. That is all very well, but do we feel that same way today? Ah, this is the important thing: Once you had the blessed assurance that you belonged to Jesus. Not only that, but you possessed that strange and wondrous knowledge that He belonged to you, that He was your Saviour. But now, as you look back, how has it been with you? Has this sweet and holy fellowship continued unbroken: your love, unaltered; your time of prayer and Bible reading, undenied? Or did you see opportunities of working for the Lord which you let slip simply through the excuse that you had something to do for yourself? Did you have opportunities of testifying for Jesus and let them go, and then found you had no testimony to give? You *knew* you were a new creature in Christ Jesus, for all things had become new. But did the new things stay new? Did they always hold the newly-discovered thrill or did you let them become secondary and commonplace? If you did, then it was because you had lost the magic touch of prayer.

If you had not drifted, your life would have been more blessed than it is today; you would have had an increased joy born of constant Christian living and fellowship with Him whose name you bear. How easy it is to drift! There are just thousands of people in this land of ours that have experienced the joy of salvation and yet have failed to obey the Scripture injunction—"Hold that fast which thou hast," and because they have failed they think Jesus has, too! But never! Jesus is as able to help you after you have failed as before you have failed—and as willing!

There *are* lots of things to hinder us in living for Jesus. Indeed it seems at times as though the whole world were against us. Not enough that the devil, enemy of every soul, should oppose us, but the old carnal nature rebels, too, for "the carnal mind is enmity against God: for it is not subject to the law of God, neither indeed can be. So then they that are in the flesh cannot please God" (Rom. 8: 7, 8). Satan opposes us, the outside world opposes us and the old Adamic nature hinders, too; but Christian friends, that is no excuse! Jesus has said, "In the world you have tribulation, but be of good cheer, I have overcome the world." And it matters not that the whole world seems to oppose, you may still stand *and*, with a great confidence in your heart, sing praises to the Lord Jesus.

The Lord allows these things to come just like a rock in the road. The wagon wheels come to the rock and find difficulty in getting over it, but once over the rock stands guard behind the wheel, keeping it from sliding back again. Every trial, when it is past, leaves its support and encouragement. It is when we lose our vision that we drift. You recall the man who took a job as sexton. He saw people being buried. At first, as he saw them being brought in, it gave him much concern. He thought about God, and wondered whether or not these people were saved. Some of them he had known; some he could have tried to win to Christ while they were yet alive. Would they have gone to a Christless grave if he had done his part in bringing them the Gospel? With every day more caskets arrived. The sexton grew less thoughtful. As the days went by the matter impressed him less and less. It seemed easier and easier for him to help in the burial. He forgot that people were dying in sin. He no longer wondered if they were saved. Finally the work became pure routine and provoked no thought in him, at all.

Herein lies a warning! Let us not grow so familiar with religion as to lose the soul-stirring and faith-increasing quality which makes it vital and precious. We are apt to say the Lord's Prayer so often and to sing hymns so frequently that we forget the meaning of any and all of them. Let us ask the Lord ever to keep before us the need souls have for salvation and our responsibility in leading them into the way.

Some people never think for a moment that it is easier to drift backward than to row forward. Some have drifted sleepily along through so many months, perchance, years, so that when, at last, they are awakened to their need, they discover it to be appalling.

On Christmas Day, about two years ago in Miami, I went out to swim one morning before breakfast. Mother had called me for my usual morning swim, but I was so sleepy! I plunged in, however, and found the water warm and still. After swimming out some little distance I lay over on my back to float. The sun made it so warm that I was just lying there enjoying myself. And I fell asleep! I certainly don't see how it could have happened, but, anyway, it *did*, and turning on my side I found I was not in bed at all—as I had thought—but under water and choking. You may be sure that I struck out energetically for the shore. Now I had drifted out quite a distance, unconsciously, before I had gone completely to sleep—and I was frightened when I wakened so suddenly! It would frighten some of you, no doubt, if you were to really awaken, today, and find how far you have drifted without knowing it, on the spiritual sea.

Some, upon discovering how they have drifted,

are afraid to stop and look back. There are so many miles between them and the Cross. There are so many miles they have departed from living in the light as Christ is in the light. Therefore, they cannot turn about to hear the voice of the preacher without being convicted, and knowing that they have been drifting all this while aimlessly and carelessly along. You can either live your life selfishly, or gloriously for the Lord. It may be easier to live a selfish life, and shabby life for the Lord, but you must put your trust in Him and go straight forward and ask the Holy Spirit to lead you, if you would live gloriously. Then you will not drift.

When they hear about "drifting America" some people say, "But America is *not* drifting." You think it to be a thing impossible for us to drift? Do you realize that Babylon and Greece and Rome drifted? And is it not possible, yea probable, that a prosperous nation, with its subsequent luxuries, shall omit the spiritual and drift toward materialism? Yes, verily, and that means death to the spiritual! Americans are getting to be ease-loving people, money-loving people, and—here is the danger—church-tolerating people. To tolerate the church instead of supporting it! America is drifting fast toward prayerlessness. Only the God-fearing, Bible-reading, prayer-offering people of this country can keep it from drifting into utter godlessness, as kingdoms of the past have drifted. Listen to the word in I Tim. 2: "I exhort, therefore, that, first of all, supplications, prayers, intercessions, and giving of thanks, be made for all men; for kings, and for all that are in authority; that we may lead a quiet and peaceable life in all godliness and honesty." For our President, for every member of the Cabinet, for every Senator, for every Congressman, for every Governor and every Mayor in these United States of America, we ought to pray. It is a safeguard against drifting.

And take heed of this: it is possible for our churches to drift, too. This day that is going into history will be regarded, by many, as a day of drifting. When a new religious awakening comes to America people are going to discuss this day, particularly with its attack upon evangelism, as a day of spiritual lethargy. When the minds of church members are on the material things continuously it is impossible that the church will not suffer. Above all things it is the duty of a minister today to stand in the pulpit and *preach the Word*. Indeed, if he has to step out of the pulpit and make the street corner his pulpit, he must preach the Word and make the people hear. He must tell the people in what direction they are going, that they must repent, as Jesus Himself told them: "Except ye repent ye shall all likewise perish." There is no substitute for the Gospel of Jesus, no cleansing so thorough, no guidance so divine, no encouragement so genuine, as that which results from the Gospel of our Lord. The fragrance and sweetness of its truth is the power which will drive out dead formalism and worldly-mindedness from any church.

If you want to see a drifting church with a few languid members gathered together on Sunday morning visit a church where there is no spirit of devotion in the congregation—where there is no sense of praise, no reading of the Word as the true inspired Bible—and you will find it drifting, right enough. And the leaders are letting the others drift on, to meet the tests and temptations of the world, without the truth they must have to overcome. Brother minister, our responsibility is great, it is our business to strengthen the weak hands, to urge them to grip the oars and turn the boat upstream. While some are drifting others are plowing upstream. No one, except he so choose, need to live a powerless, apologetic, compromising life. God is the same wonder-worker. He has not taken the Holy Spirit away from the Church. He has come to abide with us forever. Can we not claim the same power for the Church of today which the Apostolic Church knew? I believe we can.

Let us not forget the importance of the individual. Individuals make the Church, the nation. Every life has its influence upon other lives. One praying, soul-winning Christian in a single church exerts tremendous influence over the entire company. He is the "crown of rejoicing" to the minister, he is the "living epistle" to all men. When an individual member of the church begins drifting, he encourages others to do so.

Some Christians drift away from the Word. The Psalmist said, "Thy word have I hid in my heart, that I might not sin against thee." True this, then, that either "this Book will keep me from sin, or sin will keep me from this Book."

We must take the Word of God for what it is—a sure foundation. Oh, if you have drifted away from the Bible, come back again! Renew your vows! Do not drift away from the personality of Jesus nor be persuaded to accept a mere theory in its place. Do not accept untried doctrines for the ancient power of Jesus. May we not go on living, simply doing the "best we can" when we can have God's best!

Remember Peter. Like us, he is full of mistakes, very human and impulsive, but down in his heart always wanting to please the Master. But, Peter drifted—and so have we. Yet, if Peter came back, can not we?

Peter drifted away from the Lord at a most critical time, and that is usually what the rest of us do. Just a time when we ought to stand fast, we drift.

It all began with a boast, you know. And how often have our backslidings begun that way! Peter said (we have read the account from Mark 14, verse 29), "although all shall be offended," he said, "yet will not I." On the spur of the moment he had felt he could do anything in the world for Jesus. Then he suddenly lost his courage when the time came. There might have been a time when you thought it impossible that you should ever drift, and you told others so. You testified to the great satisfaction you had found in living the Christian life, and you said, "though all others turn and flee, I shall be faithful always." You boasted, not that "by His grace" you would do this or that, but simply because you were living the Christian life then you supposed you would be able always to do so. But take heed how you boast. Paul said, "I glory not save in the cross of Christ."

The next evidence of Peter's drifting is found in the thirty-seventh verse of the same chapter. Peter failed to watch and pray, and Jesus "cometh and findeth them sleeping and saith unto Peter, Simon, sleepest thou? Couldst thou not watch with me one hour?" We see the unwatchfulness and prayerlessness of Peter caused him to get farther away from the Lord, but there was another step in his drifting. It was his fleshly service, (verse 47) his doing what he thought the Lord wanted him to do for Him, and not what the Lord told him. When the soldiers came into Gethsemane to take Jesus prisoner, Peter took out his sword and struck off the ear of the High Priest's servant. Have you ever wanted to lead people away from perhaps some false doctrine: or, that is, you thought it was? And you took out a sword and not only cut off their ear with the sword but their whole head?

Sometimes intolerance of the religious views and practices of others lead to using the sword like Peter's, to the harm of everybody's conscience, rather than the Sword of the Spirit, which should be our whole defence.

But, this is not the last of Peter's drifting. We read, in the fifty-fourth verse, "Peter followed him afar off unto the high priest's palace, and went in, and sat with the servants, to see the end." What did he do? He didn't walk by the Master's side, not when Jesus' hands were in chains. He didn't walk by His side and say, "Master, can I take some message to somebody? Can I help you, Lord Jesus!" No, he followed afar off, and although he must have been silent and down-cast, yet he was walking with the crowd that was laughing and jeering and making fun of his Master, and would eventually crucify Him.

And when he got to the high priest's palace, what did he do? He stood back. He was with the soldiers and servants and warmed his hands by the fire and talked with the enemies of Jesus. What was the result? The denial of Jesus, just as He, Himself, had prophesied. Read verse sixty-eight:

"Now Peter sat without in the palace: and a damsel came unto him, saying Thou also wast with Jesus of Galilee. But he denied before them all, saying, I know not what thou sayest." "I don't know anything about salvation, I don't know anything about this Jesus you talk about. I tell you, I know nothing about this matter."

First, not prayerful and watchful, then using his sword against somebody, then he talked with the enemies of Jesus when he could have taken his stand, and at last, he denied his Lord. Surely he had drifted a long way off since he had said, "We believe and art sure thou art the Son of God."

Once you said, "I believe Jesus is the Son of God." There was a ring to your testimony, a reality behind your words. You could hardly imagine that you, yourself, could backslide. Others might fail the Lord but you would not think of doing so! Then you failed to watch and pray: because you did not watch you let sin creep in and because you did not pray it stayed in, gnawing its way into your very soul, destroying as it went. Then whatever service you rendered in the church was of your own pleasure and plan. It was fleshly service, not a result of spiritual understanding and appreciation. You followed Jesus afar off.

See how much like Peter you have been? And, at last, you found your best friends were people who didn't love your Master at all, or care anything about His Church, yet you talked their language, did the things they did, and when the subject of Christ or the Bible or religion was brought up you were diplomatic. So diplomatic, that you never spoke a word for Jesus or said a thing that might endanger your friendship with the world! You "denied the Lord that bought you" and "counted the blood of the covenant, wherewith you were sanctified, an unholy thing, and hath done despite unto the Spirit of grace?" Yes, Peter drifted! But so have you! Do not pity or condemn Peter when you have done likewise.

But, listen: Peter got back, and so can you! Stop! Put the oars straight out against the current and *come back*. The Lord will open up the way for you. He will put strength into your arms to grip the oars. The tide is strong and you have gone with it too long, but by His grace and power you can come back.

Peter stopped drifting and came back. It was probably a result of what Jesus had said when He told Peter before all this happened that he would deny Him. But even then Jesus told Peter, "Satan hath desired to have you, that he may sift you as wheat: But I have prayed for thee, that thy faith fail not." And remember this, Jesus is still the Intercessor. He is now at the right hand of God. He is making unceasing petitions for you night and day. You are never, never out of His presence. He knows your need and He will supply your need. He remembers you and is ever presenting your need before the Father's throne.

Not only the fact that Jesus said He was praying for him brought Peter back, but we read in Luke 22:61 that "the Lord turned, and looked upon Peter. And Peter remembered the word of the Lord, how he had said unto him, Before the cock crow, thou shalt deny me thrice. And Peter went out, and wept bitterly." When the Master turned those eyes of compassion, so deep and unfathomable, and looked at him, Peter remembered and went out and wept bitterly.

But, you recall what happened when Jesus came out of the grave on the resurrection morning. He sent word to the disciples, "Go tell my disciples—and Peter." *Peter!* Peter, who denied his Lord and said he didn't know anything about Him; yet when Jesus stood by the open grave He said, "Take my message to the disciples, *and Peter.*"

Notice that Peter had everything to do with his drifting away from the Lord—but it was the Lord that had everything to do with getting him back. Three things Jesus did for Peter—prayed for him before his denial, looked at him during his denial, sent a message to him after his denial. "I know your trials are heavy. Peter," He said, "But I am going to be in Galilee again. One day I passed along and said, 'Follow Me,' and you followed Me. And even though you denied Me, I have not forsaken you."

Yes, Peter would go into Galilee, as he was bidden in the Easter message—and that early morning when he saw Jesus there alone on the shore he just jumped out of the boat and swam for shore. He wasn't going to drift any more, and he had a determination to get to Jesus (we read of this in John 21:7).

When he did come Jesus questioned him three times. He had denied his Lord three and Jesus questioned him three times. "Simon, son of James, lovest thou me more than these?" And Peter said: "Yea, Lord; thou knowest that I love thee."

"Lovest thou me—Simon, son of Jonas, lovest thou me?" Indeed he did. "Simon, lovest thou me, more than those boats, more than the servants in the house of the high priest at whose fire you warmed your hands? Lovest thou me more than these?" "Lord, thou knowest all things: thou knowest that I love thee."

And what did Jesus do? He took him back at the beginning and said, "Peter, follow thou me." One day Jesus had said, "Follow me, and I will make you fishers of men." And this day He took him back to the beginning and said, "Peter, follow me." You may have drifted—all of us have at times. But He is so willing and His message to you today is that of His forgiveness, His readiness to help you and take you back, though you have drifted away from Him.

If you really stop drifting and start the Christian life over again in earnest you must have more than just a message from Jesus through somebody else. You must have a talk with Jesus Himself. He will take you back to the beginning, like He took Peter, and He will say those two words which you heard so many years ago, and which thrilled and transformed your life, "Follow Me." They still hold the same charm and brightness—yea, more to you than ever before, for you can appreciate them now. Jesus stands upon the shore. He waits for you to come to Him, as Peter came. No one has drifted so far that they cannot do that, because all you have to do is turn to Him, open your heart, confess your need, ask His forgiveness.

Just come, like Peter did. He came on the shore and there was asked, "Lovest thou me?" And if you can say, "Lord, thou knowest I love thee," not once or twice but three times and mean it more than anything else in the world, then forgiveness is yours.

Peter had not lost his faith in Jesus for the Master had prayed that his "faith fail not" . . . if he lost faith he couldn't come back and neither can you. But you still believe in Jesus' love and goodness and power to save you, don't you? You may not believe so much in yourself but that also means you have ridded yourself of that proud and boastful spirit which first started you drifting. Faith brings you back. Faith brings the drifting individual back; prayer brings the drifting nation back; Holy Spirit power brings the drifting church back. But after all, our personal relationship with Jesus Christ as individuals means more to us than anything else. If we have drifted let us repent and come back, and renew our covenant with our Lord.

Printed in the United States of America

www.ingramcontent.com/pod-product-compliance
Lightning Source LLC
Chambersburg PA
CBHW070702100426
42735CB00039B/2434